Follow Me

A STUDY ON THE GOSPEL OF MARK

ALEXA HESS

Study Suggestions

We believe that the Bible is true, trustworthy, and timeless and that it is vitally important for all believers. These study suggestions are intended to help you more effectively study Scripture as you seek to know and love God through His Word.

SUGGESTED STUDY TOOLS

- A Bible

- A double-spaced, printed copy of the Scripture passages that this study covers. You can use a website like *www.biblegateway.com* to copy the text of a passage and print out a double-spaced copy to be able to mark on easily

- A journal to write notes or prayers

- Pens, colored pencils, and highlighters

- A dictionary to look up unfamiliar words

HOW TO USE THIS STUDY

Begin your study time in prayer. Ask God to reveal Himself to you, to help you understand what you are reading, and to transform you with His Word (Psalm 119:18).

Before you read what is written in each day of the study itself, read the assigned passages of Scripture for that day. Use your double-spaced copy to circle, underline, highlight, draw arrows, and mark in any way you would like to help you dig deeper as you work through a passage.

Read the daily written content provided for the current study day.

Answer the questions that appear at the end of each study day.

The inductive method provides tools for deeper and more intentional Bible study. To study the Bible inductively, work through the steps below after reading background information on the book.

1 OBSERVATION & COMPREHENSION
Key question: What does the text say?

After reading the daily Scripture in its entirety at least once, begin working with smaller portions of the Scripture. Read a passage of Scripture repetitively, and then mark the following items in the text:

- Key or repeated words and ideas
- Key themes
- Transition words (Ex: therefore, but, because, if/then, likewise, etc.)
- Lists
- Comparisons and contrasts
- Commands
- Unfamiliar words (look these up in a dictionary)
- Questions you have about the text

2 INTERPRETATION
Key question: What does the text mean?

Once you have annotated the text, work through the following steps to help you interpret its meaning:

- Read the passage in other versions for a better understanding of the text.
- Read cross-references to help interpret Scripture with Scripture.
- Paraphrase or summarize the passage to check for understanding.
- Identify how the text reflects the metanarrative of Scripture, which is the story of creation, fall, redemption, and restoration.
- Read trustworthy commentaries if you need further insight into the meaning of the passage.

3 APPLICATION

Key Question: How should the truth of this passage change me?

Bible study is not merely an intellectual pursuit. The truths about God, ourselves, and the gospel that we discover in Scripture should produce transformation in our hearts and lives. Answer the following questions as you consider what you have learned in your study:

- What attributes of God's character are revealed in the passage?

    Consider places where the text directly states the character of God, as well as how His character is revealed through His words and actions.

- What do I learn about myself in light of who God is?

    Consider how you fall short of God's character, how the text reveals your sin nature, and what it says about your new identity in Christ.

- How should this truth change me?

    A passage of Scripture may contain direct commands telling us what to do or warnings about sins to avoid in order to help us grow in holiness. Other times our application flows out of seeing ourselves in light of God's character. As we pray and reflect on how God is calling us to change in light of His Word, we should be asking questions like, "How should I pray for God to change my heart?" and "What practical steps can I take toward cultivating habits of holiness?"

ETERNAL

God has no beginning and no end. He always was, always is, and always will be.

HAB. 1:12 / REV. 1:8 / IS. 41:4

FAITHFUL

God is incapable of anything but fidelity. He is loyally devoted to His plan and purpose.

2 TIM. 2:13 / DEUT. 7:9
HEB. 10:23

GOOD

God is pure; there is no defilement in Him. He is unable to sin, and all He does is good.

GEN. 1:31 / PS. 34:8 / PS. 107:1

GRACIOUS

God is kind, giving us gifts and benefits we do not deserve.

2 KINGS 13:23 / PS. 145:8
IS. 30:18

HOLY

God is undefiled and unable to be in the presence of defilement. He is sacred and set-apart.

REV. 4:8 / LEV. 19:2 / HAB. 1:13

INCOMPREHENSIBLE & TRANSCENDENT

God is high above and beyond human understanding. He is unable to be fully known.

PS. 145:3 / IS. 55:8-9
ROM. 11:33-36

IMMUTABLE

God does not change. He is the same yesterday, today, and tomorrow.

1 SAM. 15:29 / ROM. 11:29
JAMES 1:17

INFINITE

God is limitless. He exhibits all of His attributes perfectly and boundlessly.

ROM. 11:33-36 / IS. 40:28
PS. 147:5

JEALOUS

God is desirous of receiving the praise and affection He rightly deserves.

EX. 20:5 / DEUT. 4:23-24
JOSH. 24:19

JUST

God governs in perfect justice. He acts in accordance with justice. In Him, there is no wrongdoing or dishonesty.

IS. 61:8 / DEUT. 32:4 / PS. 146:7-9

LOVING

God is eternally, enduringly, steadfastly loving and affectionate. He does not forsake or betray His covenant love.

JN. 3:16 / EPH. 2:4-5 / 1 JN. 4:16

MERCIFUL

God is compassionate, withholding from us the wrath that we deserve.

TITUS 3:5 / PS. 25:10
LAM. 3:22-23

OMNIPOTENT

God is all-powerful; His strength is unlimited.

MAT. 19:26 / JOB 42:1-2
JER. 32:27

OMNIPRESENT

God is everywhere; His presence is near and permeating.

PROV. 15:3 / PS. 139:7-10
JER. 23:23-24

OMNISCIENT

God is all-knowing; there is nothing unknown to Him.

PS. 147:4 / I JN. 3:20
HEB. 4:13

PATIENT

God is long-suffering and enduring. He gives ample opportunity for people to turn toward Him.

ROM. 2:4 / 2 PET. 3:9 / PS. 86:15

SELF-EXISTENT

God was not created but exists by His power alone.

PS. 90:1-2 / JN. 1:4 / JN. 5:26

SELF-SUFFICIENT

God has no needs and depends on nothing, but everything depends on God.

IS. 40:28-31 / ACTS 17:24-25
PHIL. 4:19

SOVEREIGN

God governs over all things; He is in complete control.

COL. 1:17 / PS. 24:1-2
1 CHRON. 29:11-12

TRUTHFUL

God is our measurement of what is fact. By Him we are able to discern true and false.

JN. 3:33 / ROM. 1:25 / JN. 14:6

WISE

God is infinitely knowledgeable and is judicious with His knowledge.

IS. 46:9-10 / IS. 55:9 / PROV. 3:19

WRATHFUL

God stands in opposition to all that is evil. He enacts judgment according to His holiness, righteousness, and justice.

PS. 69:24 / JN. 3:36 / ROM. 1:18

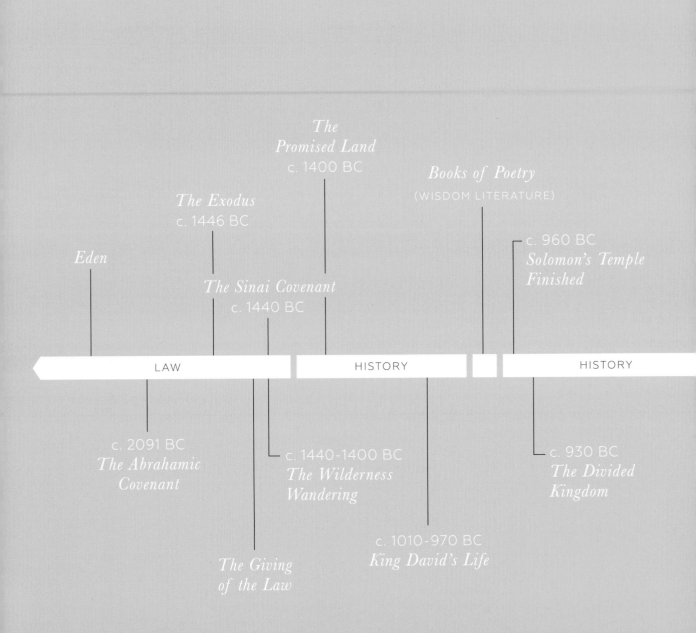

The
Promised Land
c. 1400 BC

Books of Poetry
(WISDOM LITERATURE)

The Exodus
c. 1446 BC

c. 960 BC
Solomon's Temple
Finished

Eden

The Sinai Covenant
c. 1440 BC

LAW　　　　　　　HISTORY　　　　　　HISTORY

c. 2091 BC
The Abrahamic
Covenant

c. 1440-1400 BC
The Wilderness
Wandering

c. 930 BC
The Divided
Kingdom

c. 1010-970 BC
King David's Life

The Giving
of the Law

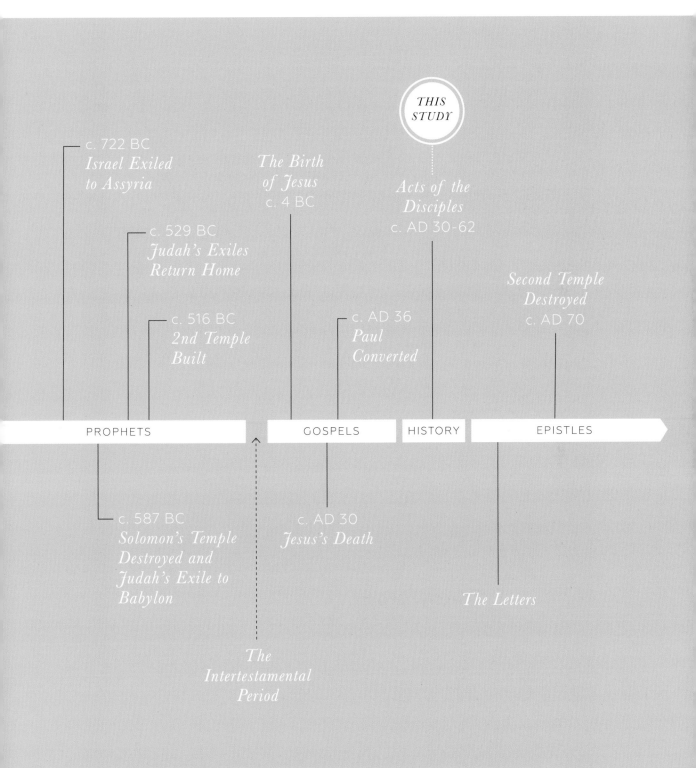

THIS
STUDY

c. 722 BC
Israel Exiled
to Assyria

The Birth
of Jesus
c. 4 BC

Acts of the
Disciples
c. AD 30-62

c. 529 BC
Judah's Exiles
Return Home

Second Temple
Destroyed
c. AD 70

c. 516 BC
2nd Temple
Built

c. AD 36
Paul
Converted

PROPHETS

GOSPELS

HISTORY

EPISTLES

c. 587 BC
Solomon's Temple
Destroyed and
Judah's Exile to
Babylon

c. AD 30
Jesus's Death

The Letters

The
Intertestamental
Period

Creation

In the beginning, God created the universe. He made the world and everything in it. He created humans in His own image to be His representatives on the earth.

Fall

The first humans, Adam and Eve, disobeyed God by eating from the fruit of the Tree of Knowledge of Good and Evil. Their disobedience impacted the whole world. The punishment for sin is death, and because of Adam's original sin, all humans are sinful and condemned to death.

Redemption

God sent His Son to become a human and redeem His people. Jesus Christ lived a sinless life but died on the cross to pay the penalty for sin. He resurrected from the dead and ascended into heaven. All who put their faith in Jesus are saved from death and freely receive the gift of eternal life.

Restoration

One day, Jesus Christ will return again and restore all that sin destroyed. He will usher in a new heaven and new earth where all who trust in Him will live eternally with glorified bodies in the presence of God.

Readers can view the Gospel of Mark
as a mosaic, in which each piece
comes together to create
a full picture of Jesus Christ.

Contents

Places of Jesus's Ministry

GALILEE & CAPERNAUM

Mark 1–4, 9:30, 9:33

**THE DISTRICT
OF DALMANUTHA**

Mark 8:10

GERASENES

Mark 5:1

CAESAREA PHILIPPI

Mark 8:27

NAZARETH

Mark 6:1

MOUNT TABOR

Mark 9:2–13

BETHSAIDA

Mark 6:45, 8:22

JUDEA

Mark 10:1

GENNESARET

Mark 6:53

JERICHO

Mark 10:46

TYRE

Mark 7:24

BETHANY

Mark 14:3–11

SEA OF GALILEE

Mark 7:31

JERUSALEM

Mark 11–14:2, 14:12–16

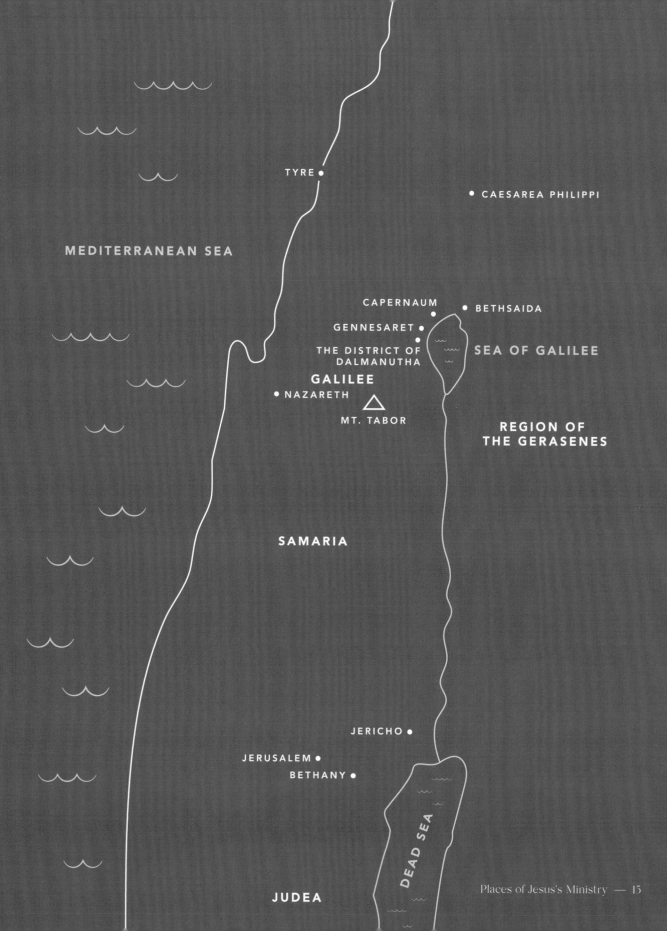

TYRE •

• CAESAREA PHILIPPI

MEDITERRANEAN SEA

CAPERNAUM •
• BETHSAIDA

GENNESARET •

THE DISTRICT OF
DALMANUTHA

SEA OF GALILEE

GALILEE

• NAZARETH

△

MT. TABOR

**REGION OF
THE GERASENES**

SAMARIA

JERICHO •

JERUSALEM •

BETHANY •

DEAD SEA

JUDEA

Throughout the Gospel of Mark,
Mark emphasizes Christ's
authority and identity.

A Divine Mosaic

READ MARK 1–16

An artist gathers his pieces of colored glass. One by one, he slowly begins to put the pieces together—each piece purposeful, each piece necessary. Up close, the glass appears to be only a pile, but as each piece is placed, a picture begins to form. At last, the artist places his final piece of glass and steps back from his work. As he steps back, we are able to see the fullness of the desired picture. Each small piece of glass has formed the image of Jesus Christ.

In this scenario, this artist is none other than Mark. Mark's approach to his Gospel account is to take pieces of Jesus's story—the aspects of His life, death, and resurrection—and arrange the pieces in such a way that one has a complete understanding of who Christ is and what He did. Therefore, readers can view the Gospel of Mark as a mosaic, in which each piece comes together to create a full picture of Jesus Christ.

Little is known about Mark. In fact, the Gospel of Mark does not once reference Mark. However, from church tradition, we learn that Mark is John Mark, who appears in the book of Acts. Mark accompanied Barnabas and Paul on their first missionary journey and was a close companion to the Apostle Peter. Church history affirms that Mark was a secretary and translator for Peter and that the primary source for Mark's Gospel was Peter. It is said that Mark penned his Gospel near the end of Peter's life, so it is likely that the Gospel of Mark was written in the mid to late 50s in Rome. Through Peter's testimony, Mark gathered accounts of Jesus's ministry and pieced them together to form the Gospel of Mark.

The Gospel of Mark is the shortest of the four gospels. Each chapter moves quickly, pulling the reader into a fast-paced and exciting account of Christ. Unlike other gospel accounts that contain longer accounts and descriptions, the Gospel of Mark is simple and to the point. The brevity of Mark allows the reader to be able to move straight to the heart of Jesus's teaching and identity.

Mark wrote his Gospel for Roman Christians undergoing persecution under Nero, the emperor of Rome who was against Christianity. Mark wrote for Gentiles, or non-Jews, which explains why Mark does not quote very much from the Old Testament and why he explains Jewish customs throughout the book. His intention to speak to this particular audience explains Mark's purpose in painting a portrait of Christ. Christians experiencing persecution could be encouraged by an account that reminded them of who they were being persecuted for and why this persecution was worthwhile. These Christians were not being persecuted for following an ordinary man—they were following the Son of God.

From the very first sentence of Mark, we learn the emphasis of Mark's Gospel: Jesus Christ is the Son of God. Throughout the Gospel of Mark, Mark emphasizes Christ's authority and identity. The Gospel speaks primarily to what Jesus did, presenting Him as a man of action whose divinity and authority were displayed through His healings and miracles. As we journey through Mark, we see how Jesus moved toward those who were afflicted and in need, using His divine power to forgive sins and provide restoration from disease and death.

Throughout Mark's Gospel, we see repeating themes of discipleship and faith. Jesus's discipleship amongst the twelve disciples gives a model for us as believers today in our own discipleship. Throughout Mark, we not only see what true discipleship looks like but what true faith looks like. True discipleship and faith are presented as following Jesus, not because He is a moral teacher but because He is the Son of God. Through the disciples' accounts, as well as other encounters with people, we learn how true faith involves placing belief and trust in who Jesus is, even if we do not always understand how Jesus works. Faith in Christ and being a disciple of Christ not only involves following Christ but participating

in His mission. As believers today, we join the disciples in participating in Christ's mission by spreading the good news of salvation and being people who reflect the qualities of Christ.

In Mark, we also see the theme of insiders and outsiders. This theme emphasizes how followers of Christ were often not the elite but those who were considered outsiders like women, Gentiles, and "unclean" Jews. These people were meek and recognized their need for Christ.

Thus, the outsiders became the insiders, revealing how Christ's invitation for salvation is best received by those who are humble in heart. What a message for those of us today who think that our works, status, or knowledge earn us a place in God's kingdom. True faith in Christ is an understanding that we cannot do anything on our own to earn salvation and that we need Jesus. Those in Mark's Gospel recognized their complete need for Christ, and so should we. Nothing else can save us but the blood of Christ, given to us by grace through faith.

From start to finish, Mark's Gospel causes us to fix our eyes on Christ. Whether you have walked with Jesus for a while or are new in the faith, allow yourself to read what Jesus did with fresh eyes. And then allow yourself to marvel at who Jesus is, rejoicing in the Son of God who made a way for you to experience true and everlasting life.

From start to finish,
Mark's Gospel causes us to
fix our eyes on Christ.

Day One — Questions

What key words or themes stood out to you from reading Mark?

What did you learn about Christ's identity and character from reading Mark?

What is something that Christ did throughout His ministry that stands out to you the most?

What is Faith?

Because one of the dominant themes in Mark's Gospel is faith, it is important to understand from the start of this study what faith is. Our world uses the word "faith" in different ways. When facing a difficult opposition, someone might say, "Just have faith!" When someone is having a hard time trusting another, the other person might say, "Have faith in me!" Yet Biblical faith involves something different than this general faith we might throw around in our language.

What is Biblical Faith?

Biblical faith involves three elements that cannot be divorced from one another: knowledge, belief, and trust.

KNOWLEDGE

Knowledge involves knowing who God is. And how can we know who God is? One of the best ways we can grow in our knowledge of God is by reading His Word. The Bible is the inerrant, sufficient, and eternal Word of God, and when we study it, we discover unchanging truths about God's character and His plan for redemption. These truths have the power to transform us and grow our faith.

BELIEF

Faith does not just involve knowing about God and His Word but also believing God and His Word to be true. Many people may have abundant knowledge about God and Scripture, but they do not believe God and His Word are true. Biblical faith believes that God is who He says He is and that His Word is true and reliable. Hebrews 11:6 tells us, "Now without faith it is impossible to please God, since the one who draws near to him must believe that he exists..." Belief in God fuels our faith.

TRUST

Coupled with knowledge and belief is trust. Trust involves placing our confidence and hope in Jesus. Faith is trusting Jesus as our Savior and the only One who can forgive our sin. Trust also involves submitting to Jesus as Lord and being obedient to Him. When we place our faith in Jesus, we are dedicating our lives in faithful service to Him because of what He has done for us.

Faith That Saves Us

These three aspects of faith are what is described as "saving faith." In order for some-one to be saved, they must know who God is and what His Word says, believe God and His Word to be true, and trust Jesus as their Savior. Yet saving faith is not possi-ble without the grace and power of God. In John 6:44, Jesus says, "No one can come to me unless the Father who sent me draws him." Without God's grace, no one can be saved. The ability to know, believe, and trust is a gift granted by God's grace through the power of the Holy Spirit.

So, are we saved by God's grace or our own faith? While our salvation is grounded in the grace of Christ alone, faith is the vehicle by which this grace is received. Although saving faith can be difficult to fully grasp, we should be careful not to overthink our personal faith. The question we should be asking in regards to our salvation is not "Do I have a strong enough faith?" but rather "Do I believe Jesus is who He says He is?" While knowledge, belief, and trust are all important elements of saving faith, it is trust in Jesus that gives us security in our salvation. If we say we trust in Jesus and live our lives in obedience to Him, we can be confident that we have been saved.

Faith That Sustains Us

Our faith does not stop after we have been saved. The Christian life is a continual walk of faith. Each day, we are to place our confidence and hope in God and what His Word says. We are to live out the salvation we have received through obedience to the Lord. Just as God gives us grace for the faith that saves us, He also gives us grace for the faith that sustains us. Through the power of the Holy Spirit, we receive the strength we need to live out our faith. Even if we struggle in our obedience or wrestle with doubt, the Holy Spirit helps us rest in Christ's grace and remain firm in our faith. With the guidance of the Spirit, we daily walk by faith as we trust in the God who saves and sustains us.

Jesus Christ not only brings the gospel;
He is the One who fulfills the gospel.

Son of God

READ MARK 1:1–20

Mark starts his Gospel with a sentence that defines the message of his account: "The beginning of the gospel of Jesus Christ, the Son of God." While other Gospels like Matthew and Luke begin with Christ's birth story, Mark begins his Gospel with a declaration of Christ's identity. This book is all about Jesus Christ, the Son of God.

The word "gospel" in verse 1 means "good news." Mark has designated that this good news is the good news of Jesus Christ. This message is the story of salvation, and Jesus is the main character. Jesus Christ not only brings the gospel; He is the One who fulfills the gospel. He is the embodiment of the good news that has come to earth. As the Son of God, Jesus is the One who accomplishes salvation and brings salvation for those who trust and believe in Him.

Mark also opens his Gospel with a quotation from Isaiah 40:3, which foretells the ministry of John the Baptist. Through this prophecy, Mark teaches how John the Baptist is a messenger of the gospel, but he is not the One whom the gospel is about. Isaiah 40:3 reveals that John the Baptist's mission is to prepare the way for the Messiah. However, John is not just preparing the way for the Messiah; he is preparing the way for God. The promised Messiah spoken throughout the prophets is the Son of God — God in the flesh.

In verse 7, John is clear that he pales in comparison to the power of the One who is coming. John declares that he may baptize people with water, but this man to come will baptize people with the Holy Spirit. By this statement, John reveals how this coming One is no ordinary man. It is only God who can provide salvation and the power of the Holy Spirit.

Through Christ's baptism, we learn how the One John speaks about is Jesus Christ. When Jesus is baptized by John, something miraculous happens. As Christ comes up from the water, the heavens open, the Spirit descends on Christ, and God's voice declares that Jesus is His Son, in whom He is well pleased. John used his voice to proclaim Christ's identity, and God's voice confirms Christ's identity. There is no disputing the voice of God, for what God declares is the truth. Jesus Christ is the Son of God.

Jesus's temptation in the wilderness tests His identity as Son of God. Will He be like Israel, who wandered forty days in the wilderness, opposing God and falling into sin? Or will He resist temptation and remain obedient to God? Mark and other Gospel accounts reveal that Satan tempted Jesus for forty days, but Jesus did not give in to his temptation. As God in the flesh, Jesus has the power to resist Satan's temptation, and therefore, He holds power over Satan himself.

After His baptism and temptation in the wilderness, Jesus declares His identity as the Son of God by proclaiming the good news of salvation, saying that God's kingdom has come near. For God's kingdom to be near means that the invitation to become members in the kingdom of God is available—and it is God Himself who brings this invitation. Jesus also explains how to be brought into the kingdom of God: repent and believe. Christ's gospel invitation is simple. Jesus does not say that we must clean ourselves up to belong to God. He does not say that we must follow all the rules perfectly. He simply calls us to repent and believe. All we must do to receive salvation is turn from our sin and believe in Jesus Christ.

As Jesus calls His first disciples, we also see His authority and identity displayed. All Jesus says to the four fishermen is "follow me," and they immediately obey. The immediacy of the disciples' decision speaks to the authority Jesus possesses. He only had to say a few words, but it was the impact of the One who said the words that made all the difference. The disciples trusted who Jesus was enough to leave their entire lives behind and follow Him.

The gospel is a message of sweet simplicity, yet it requires faith. The disciples did not need to know all the answers beforehand to trust Jesus; they simply trusted Him. Their faith was small and would continue to be shaped as they followed Christ, but Jesus's character was enough for them to take the leap of faith. This begs the question: is knowing who Jesus is enough for us to place our faith in Him? Mark will soon show us Jesus's power through His acts, but it is not the acts that should cause us to believe. Who Jesus is should cause us to believe.

Even those of us who have been walking with Jesus for a while can benefit from remembering where true faith lies. Sometimes, we feel as if we need all the answers before we can trust Jesus. We feel like we need to know what He is doing and how He will accomplish what we need before we can place our trust in Him. But true faith surrenders the need for control and comfort in order to move forward. If we truly believe Jesus is who He says He is, we can place our lives in His hands. Jesus Christ is the Son of God. He is the manifestation of God's love, mercy, grace, and glory. The One who beckons to us to follow Him is no ordinary person; He is God Himself, so we can trust Him with every step that we take.

True faith surrenders
the need for control and comfort
in order to move forward.

Day Two — Questions

Why is it important for us as believers to know who Jesus is?

How do you struggle with believing who Jesus is? How can this passage, as well as the truth of God's Word, help you believe?

Consider who the disciples were when Jesus called them. What does this say about who can follow Jesus? How does this encourage you?

Only Jesus can cleanse us,
free us, and satisfy the
longing of our hearts.

One Who Had Authority

READ MARK 1:21–2:17

Mark has revealed to us Christ's identity as the Son of God. We have seen His glory displayed and His power portrayed through His baptism, temptation, and ministry call. While Christ's words, John the Baptist's words, and God's words have declared who Jesus is, it is not only words but actions that provide evidence that Jesus is the Son of God. By His actions of teaching, healing, and forgiving, Christ reveals to those around Him both His identity and authority as the Son of God, as well as His ministry mission.

Christ's first action that declares His authority is His teaching. As Jesus teaches in the synagogue, the people who gathered to listen are astonished. The people realize that Jesus teaches as One who has authority, unlike the scribes. Because the scribes were interpreters of the Law, they had derived authority, but Jesus has divine authority. The people noticed that Jesus taught not as if He was interpreting the Law but as the One who wrote the Law. And they were correct. God Himself was speaking the words He put in the minds and mouths of the authors of Scripture. He wrote the words; therefore, He has the authority to speak His words.

The second action that declares Christ's authority is when He drives out a demon. As the demon looks at Jesus, he declares, "I know who you are—the Holy One of God!" (Mark 1:24). This statement is not a confession of faith but rather a confession of identity. The demons recognize who Jesus is, even if they do not follow Him. Jesus then demonstrates His identity as the Holy One of God as He drives out the demon from the helpless man. By the words of His mouth, Jesus commands the demon to leave, and by His power, the demon obeys. Those who watch the spectacle wonder at His authority to command unclean spirits. By this exorcism, Jesus declares His authority over demons, and therefore, His authority over evil and darkness.

Third, Jesus declares His authority over sickness, disease, and disorder. Jesus heals Simon's mother-in-law, as well as a crowd of people ridden with illness or possessed by demons. Jesus also heals a man with leprosy and a man who is paralyzed. What makes the account of the paralytic man interesting, however, is that Jesus first forgives the man's sins before healing his body. The Pharisees are aghast, questioning how Jesus can forgive sins when only God can forgive sins. By these questions, the Pharisees answer their own question. Only God can forgive sins; therefore, Jesus is

God. Jesus's decision to forgive this man's sins reveals that the Son of Man not only has the ability but also the authority to forgive sin. The only One who can truly forgive our sin is the One we have sinned against. Only God can forgive us of the sin we have committed against Him.

Through Jesus's actions, Jesus reveals His authority as the Son of God to heal, forgive, and liberate, but Christ's actions also reveal what His ministry will be about. Jesus will use His time to help and move toward those who are considered outsiders. Throughout this passage, we see Jesus help a man with an unclean spirit, an unclean leper, and a man with infirmity. But Jesus also calls a tax collector to follow Him, and He is seen dining with sinners and tax collectors. Those who witness Jesus's decision to be among the rejected and despised question His actions, but Jesus replies, "It is not those who are well who need a doctor, but those who are sick. I didn't come to call the righteous, but sinners" (Mark 2:17).

In other words, Jesus has come to help those who recognize they are in need. Unlike the Pharisees or others who do not think they need anything from Jesus, the sick, the hurting, the broken, and the bruised are aware of their need for help. While Christ's message of salvation is available to all, Mark shows us how the ones who listen most to Christ's message are the ones who recognize their need for Jesus.

As we think about Christ's authority and the purpose of His mission, we too are reminded of our need for Jesus. Only Jesus can cleanse us, free us, and satisfy the longing of our hearts. Because Jesus is God, He is the solution for our sins and sufferings. God is the One who created us; therefore, He knows what we need to be whole: Himself. We may turn to people or created things to make us feel whole, but those things only leave us more broken. They may bring satisfaction, joy, or help in the moment, but soon the feelings fade, and we are right back in need.

What makes Jesus significant is that His healing and forgiveness run deep. Christ's grace is not a surface-level cleansing—His grace cleanses us down to our very core. This is why Jesus forgave the paralytic's sins before healing his body. Jesus recognized what this man needed most, which was forgiveness from the sin that separated him from God.

This is what Jesus does for us as well. By His grace, Christ restores our brokenness, heals our deepest wounds, and liberates us from our bondage to sin. And then, out of His forgiveness and grace, Christ begins to chip away at everything else. Once Jesus has taken care of our greatest need—salvation—Jesus then begins to help us with our other needs. He helps us tear down the idols to which we have been clinging, helps us conquer our fears and temptations, and helps us with our obedience as we seek to worship God. And just like everyone in today's reading, Jesus provides healing and help all by His own love, mercy, and grace. Jesus is both willing and able to give us the grace we need to experience true and lasting life.

> Christ's grace is not a surface-level cleansing — His grace cleanses us *down to our very core.*

Day Three — Questions

Consider the leper's words to Jesus in Mark 1:40. How do you struggle to believe that Jesus is *willing* to help you, not just able to help you?

What surface-level modes of comfort, help, and satisfaction are you turning to instead of Jesus? What needs to change so that you go to Him for deep and lasting care?

How does Jesus's ability and authority to forgive sin move you toward Him in the times you sin and are disobedient to God?

Salvation is not found in doing works
but in surrendering from works.

Lord of the Sabbath

READ MARK 2:18–3:6

Throughout the first few chapters of Mark, we have received multiple examples of Christ's divinity and authority. While the previous passages demonstrated Christ's identity through miracles, today's passage demonstrates Christ's identity mainly through discourse. Jesus is confronted head-on by the Pharisees, and through these interactions, Jesus proclaims the powerful truth of His identity. Jesus is not only the Son of God; He is also Lord of the Sabbath.

Before Jesus reveals His identity as Lord of the Sabbath, Jesus is confronted over the topic of fasting. Jesus is asked why His disciples do not fast while John the Baptist's disciples and the Pharisees do. While fasting was not a legal requirement, in Jesus's day, fasting had been associated with religious piety. So while fasting was not a requirement, the people questioning Jesus expected His followers to fast, just like other religious groups did.

Yet Jesus says that there is no need for His disciples to fast because they are not in a time of mourning but a time of celebration. He compares His disciples to wedding guests and Himself as the bridegroom. In the New Testament, weddings were a week-long event full of food, joy, and celebration. Weddings were a time for feasting, not fasting. Once the bridegroom left the wedding, the celebration and feasting ended, but as long as he was with them, the celebration continued. By this imagery, Jesus describes how there is no need for His disciples to fast because they are with the presence of God—and that is a reason to celebrate. But one day, Jesus will leave them, and at that time, they will fast in mourning.

Jesus's response demonstrates two important truths. First, Jesus as the bridegroom confirms His identity as God. Throughout the Old Testament, wedding imagery was used to describe God's relationship with His people. Therefore, identifying Himself as the bridegroom places Jesus as sharing the same identity as God. Second, the imagery of the bridegroom being taken away foretells Christ's death, resurrection, and future ascension. Jesus alludes to the fact that He will not remain with His disciples forever, but soon He will die, be raised, and ascend back to the Father.

The Pharisees then confront Jesus about the Sabbath. While Jesus and His disciples are walking through a grainfield, the disciples pluck some grain to eat. The Pharisees nearby see this action and confront Jesus about His disciples. To pluck grain was considered reaping, and reaping is not allowed on the Sabbath, the day of rest. The Pharisees seek to charge the disciples for not abiding by the Law, but they are unprepared for Jesus's response. Jesus tells the story of when David and his men were hungry, so they entered the temple and ate the bread of the Presence, which was bread reserved for the priests alone (1 Samuel 21:1–6). By referencing David, Jesus indirectly reveals Himself to be the anticipated Messiah who would come from David's line. As the promised royal Son of David, Jesus has authority that supersedes David; therefore, Jesus has authority over all things, including the Law.

Jesus then backs up His claim with two revolutionary statements. First, Jesus says that the Sabbath was made for man and not man for the Sabbath. The Sabbath was instituted by God to bring rest to His people, to bless them, and to give them restoration and peace. But the Pharisees had made the Sabbath a burden to honor, as they added more Sabbath laws to abide by. Through Jesus's statement, Jesus exposes the main purpose of the Sabbath. God did not create man to be enslaved by the Sabbath but to have freedom through the Sabbath. Second, Jesus claims that the Son of Man is Lord of the Sabbath. Here, Jesus asserts Himself to be the fulfillment of Sabbath rest. Sabbath rest is meant to point to Jesus, who brings us full and everlasting rest.

By declaring Himself as Lord of the Sabbath, Jesus exposes the Pharisees for their misguided thinking. The principle of the Sabbath—to worship God, enjoy rest, and love others—was being overlooked by the Pharisees' demands to follow the Law perfectly. Jesus's healing of the man in Mark 3:1–5 demonstrates this idea further. The Pharisees saw healing a man as a breach of the Sabbath, but Jesus saw healing a man as the purpose of the Sabbath. Jesus chooses to do good on the Sabbath, even if that means "breaking" the Sabbath rules.

As we look deeper, Jesus's claims reveal how the Pharisees saw their rule-abiding as a way to earn favor and acceptance with God. But as Lord of the Sabbath, Jesus reveals the true way to find acceptance with God. Salvation is not found in doing works but in surrendering from works. We do not work to earn favor with God because Christ did the work for us by dying on the cross. Through no work of our own but by receiving Christ's grace and trusting in Him, we are saved and accepted by God. We rest from our works as we rest in the finished work of Christ.

As Lord of the Sabbath, Jesus invites us to lay down our strivings and come to Him for rest (Matthew 11:28). Jesus removes the burden of obedience through works and gives us the freedom to obey and worship God—not as an obligation but as a joyful response to His grace and mercy. Working to please God brings weariness and worry, but resting in Christ's grace brings freedom and peace. We may still struggle at times to feel like we have to obey God perfectly for Him to love us or that we have to do everything right in order to secure our salvation. In these moments, we must remember Jesus, whose grace assures us that we have full acceptance and eternal salvation. For the believer, there is no burden of obligation—only freedom and rest in Christ.

As Lord of the Sabbath, Jesus invites us to lay down our strivings and come to Him for rest.

Day Four — Questions

In what ways do you struggle with feeling like you need to do the right things in order to please God? How does the gospel speak to these feelings?

How does the grace and mercy we have received through Christ motivate our obedience to God?

Read Matthew 11:28. What burdens can you give to Jesus so that you can experience His rest?

We are united with the God who created us
and saved us — a sweet and powerful
union that can never be broken.

Who Are My Mother & My Brothers?

READ MARK 3:7–35

Jesus's miracles and interactions with the Pharisees have made Jesus well-known. Word has spread about this man who can heal and drive out demons, causing large crowds to pursue and follow Him. As Jesus's ministry grows more public, Jesus officially appoints twelve disciples to share in His ministry. Jesus gives these men the authority to preach the message of the gospel and even drive out demons. And while these disciples, as well as other curious people, have chosen to follow Jesus, not everyone agrees or affirms Christ's ministry and authority. In this passage, we see two groups of people who oppose Jesus, and through these interactions, we learn who are true followers of Christ.

Jesus's family is the first to disagree with His ministry. They witness Jesus ministering to large crowds and believe He is out of His mind for teaching and interacting with so many people (Mark 3:21). His family even seeks to restrain Him and prevent Jesus from continuing with His ministry. Jesus's family's response reveals how there will be people who do not understand why Jesus is doing what He is doing, and there will be others who even try to stop Jesus and prevent Him from continuing His ministry.

These types of people cause us to think about those who question or oppose Christianity today. As believers, we will face opposition and persecution for our faith. This persecution can be as extreme as being hurt or jailed for being a Christian, or it can be less extreme, such as a harsh comment against us. When we interact with such people, we can follow the example of Jesus, who did not quit, even when He was opposed or questioned. Our faith can remain strong, even if people disagree with us or place themselves against us.

The scribes are the second group who disagree with Jesus. They accuse Jesus of being possessed by a demon, and they claim that the only reason Jesus has the power to drive out demons is because He Himself is possessed. The scribes say that He is possessed by "Beelzebul," a title that represents the prince of demons—Satan. Jesus reveals the error of the scribes' argument by telling them how Satan cannot drive out Satan. He uses an example of a divided house and kingdom to teach how a divided house or kingdom cannot stand. If Satan was divided against himself, his power would be threatened, and his schemes would be ruined.

Jesus also uses a short parable about a person tying up a strong owner of a home to describe what He has come to do. Jesus has not come to work with or by the power of Satan but to defeat Satan. Jesus has come to tear down Satan's kingdom and to establish the kingdom of God. This picture of Jesus breaking into Satan's domain and binding Him foreshadows what will ultimately be accomplished through Jesus's death and resurrection. The powerful Son of God has come to defeat sin and death and bring people freedom from Satan's grip.

The scribes' words to Jesus cause Jesus to bring them a warning in verses 28–30. Jesus says that all people who believe in Him will be forgiven, with the exception of those who commit the eternal sin. This passage of Scripture has caused much confusion and fear amongst believers, and therefore, it must be handled carefully. The eternal sin Jesus speaks of is committed by those who verbally and continually speak against the Holy Spirit with malicious intent. By verbally saying that Jesus is doing the work of the devil, the scribes were resisting the work of the Holy Spirit. Knowingly, willingly, and persistently speaking against the Spirit and His works reveals a hardened heart, a heart that has not been transformed by the gospel. A person with a hardened heart that has not been transformed by Christ's grace will not receive God's forgiveness when they stand before Him one day. Believers in Christ can never commit the eternal sin because we have been saved through Christ, and we have the power of the Spirit who keeps us from ever committing such sin.

In contrast, Jesus reveals who true believers of Christ are. In verses 33–35, Jesus says those who do the will of God are His mothers, brothers, and sisters. Instead of those who harden their hearts, true believers are those who love God and desire to do God's will. In Luke 8:21, Jesus says, "My mother and my brothers are those who hear and do the word of God." Those who belong to the family of God not only hear what God's Word says, but through the power of the Holy Spirit, they also do what God's Word says. The language of "brothers," "mother," and "sisters" also shows us the kind of union believers share with Christ. When we enter into a saving relationship with Christ, we are brought into God's family. This intimacy and union is deeper and closer than the bond of blood relationships. We are united with the God who created us and saved us—a sweet and powerful union that can never be broken.

Because of our relationship with Jesus, we have been declared children of God. While it is hard to see people on the outside who oppose the gospel and resist the power of God, it is a blessing to be on the inside, to remain in an unbreakable union with Christ. Daily we are blessed to have a heavenly Father who cares for and loves us. And out of a response to being in God's family, we obey God joyfully and faithfully. Being a child of God is a precious gift of grace.

Being a child of God is *a precious gift of grace.*

Day Five — Questions

How does Christ's mission to overthrow Satan encourage you when you struggle with sin and temptation?

How does belonging to the family of God encourage you when you are persecuted for your faith? Consider Matthew 5:10–12.

How can you remain steadfast in your faith when others question or oppose what you believe?

When the scribes who were Pharisees saw that he was eating with sinners and tax collectors, they asked his disciples, "Why does he eat with tax collectors and sinners?" When Jesus heard this, he told them, "It is not those who are well who need a doctor, but those who are sick. I didn't come to call the righteous, but sinners."

MARK 2:16–17

Week One — Reflection

Summarize the main points from this week's Scripture readings.

What did you observe from this week's passages about God and His character?

What do this week's passages reveal about the condition of mankind and yourself?

How do these passages point to the gospel?

How should you respond to these passages? What specific action steps can you take this week to apply them in your life?

Write a prayer in response to your study of God's Word. Adore God for who He is, confess sins He revealed in your own life, ask Him to empower you to walk in obedience, and pray for anyone who comes to mind as you study.

Being rooted in God's Word
enables us to bear fruit.

Sowing the Word

A good teacher tailors her material to meet the current needs of her students. She not only teaches her students what they *generally* need to know, but she also teaches them what they *specifically* need to know based on each student's learning level and comprehension. In Mark 4:1–20, Jesus utilizes a parable as His main teaching method. Parables are allegorical stories that typically teach one central message, and they normally adopt situations and imagery that would connect directly with the audience's experiences. Through this parable, Jesus teaches the value of truly listening to and living out the Word of God.

In Mark 4:10–12, Jesus describes how not everyone will understand the message of His parables. Jesus reveals how His twelve disciples, as well as others who have chosen to follow Him, have received the secret of the kingdom of God. Because they believe and trust in Jesus, they are given understanding about who God is and the workings of His kingdom. Jesus quotes from Isaiah 6:9–10 to show how those on the outside do not have this same understanding. They may look and listen, but they do not actually take in the words they hear. If they actually perceived and understood Jesus's words and the message inside the parables, they would recognize their need for Jesus and accept the forgiveness He offers.

In His parable, Jesus describes a sower and seeds. In this parable, the sower is God, who spreads the message of the gospel through His Word, Jesus. Jesus presents four different scenarios that represent four different types of people who listen to Jesus's words. In the first scenario, the sower spreads seeds on an open path where the birds quickly come and devour the seeds. These seeds represent people with hardened hearts, who are quick to shut out the message of the gospel before it has a chance to even sink into their minds.

In the second scenario, the sower sows seeds on the rocky ground. These seeds grow quickly but then wither away quickly, representing people who have an emotional response to the gospel but do not root themselves in the truth of the gospel. Because their reaction was quick and rooted in their feelings, once distress comes to shake their feelings, they abandon their faith.

In the third scenario, the sower sows seeds amongst thorns that quickly choke the message. These seeds represent people who respond to the gospel but care too much about the things of this world to dedicate their lives to Jesus. Lastly, the sower sows seeds on good ground, and the seeds grow to produce lasting fruit. These seeds represent those who hear the gospel and respond to the gospel. Unlike those before them, they receive the gospel with joy, but they also remain so rooted in its truth that troubling circumstances or worldly desires fail to hinder their growth.

The fourth scenario is an example of genuine faith in Christ. Followers of Jesus are those who hear the gospel, accept and believe the gospel, and live out the gospel. All the other seeds failed in one or more of these areas. The first seed refused to hear, the second seed heard but did not take the gospel to heart, and the third seed likely heard and possibly believed but failed to live the gospel out. The distinguishing factor amongst these examples of seeds is the fact that the fourth seed grew and produced fruit. Jesus says in John 15:8, "My Father is glorified by this: that you produce much fruit and prove to be my disciples."

Disciples of Christ produce fruit. To produce fruit means to practically live out the gospel in our everyday lives through actions of obedience to the Lord. However, even if we have heard and accepted the gospel, it can still be difficult to live out the gospel. We can act in similar ways to the other seeds by shutting out God's Word to pursue our own desires, struggling to make sacrifices for the Lord, or only trusting Jesus when life is easy.

But even though we can find ourselves falling into these habits, we have the Holy Spirit inside of us who helps us. The Spirit gives us spiritual eyes and ears that allow us to listen to and obey God's Word. His power inside of us propels us in obedience to the Lord and enables us to bear fruit.

One of the ways the Spirit helps us bear fruit for the Lord is by keeping us rooted in the Bible. The other seeds in the parable Jesus presented did not ground themselves in God's Word. As believers, we need to be daily rooted in God's Word. We need to come back to the Bible again and again, meditate on what Scripture says, and put into practice the Word of God. Being rooted in God's Word enables us to bear fruit. When we remain rooted in Scripture, we will listen to God's Word instead of shutting it out. We will persevere in affliction. We will put Jesus and His kingdom first before all else.

True listening involves living out what we hear, and the only way we can continue to listen and obey the Lord is by remaining rooted in His Word and relying on the Spirit. We must remain active listeners of God's Word by being doers of the Word and not hearers only (James 1:21–22). We must guard against the enemy and the desires of this world that seek to choke our fruitfulness. By God's grace, we have been given spiritual ears to listen to and heed God's Word, so let us allow the Word of God that has been implanted in us to flourish and bear fruit for God's glory.

Let us allow the Word of God that has been implanted in us to flourish and bear fruit for God's glory.

44

Day One — Questions

Review the four scenarios Jesus described in Mark 4:3—8. How do you see yourself struggling in similar ways to the seeds of the first three scenarios?

What does it look like to be true and active listeners of God's Word? How can you continue to be an active listener to what God's Word says and teaches?

Read Galatians 5:16—25. How do we produce fruit according to this passage? What does this look like practically in your everyday life?

The light of Christ cannot be extinguished.
His glory and truth will shine
through no matter what.

The Secret of the Kingdom

Jesus has been teaching the people parables, and in today's passage, Jesus continues to teach through three more parables. Similar to the previous passage, Jesus imploys sowing imagery in His teaching. However, unlike the prior parable that was focused on the Word of God, the parables Jesus teaches today focus on the kingdom of God. Jesus has told His disciples how the secret of the kingdom of God has been given to them (Mark 4:11), and in this passage, Jesus reveals the details of such a secret.

Before going into the sowing parables, Jesus gives a parable about a lamp. Jesus describes how no one lights a lamp to then place the lamp under a basket or a bed. A lamp is meant to be placed on a lampstand to illuminate the room. In the same way, Jesus is a lamp who has come not to be covered but to be elevated and illuminated. Jesus has come to illuminate truth in the darkness of the world. But the people's unbelief and failure to listen to Jesus's words act as a basket that covers the light of His truth.

However, the light of Christ cannot be extinguished. His glory and truth will shine through no matter what. Soon this display of glory and truth will shine brightly when Christ is resurrected. But for now, all people have the opportunity in the present to experience the light of Christ bursting through the darkness—all they have to do is listen. Those who want to understand the truth Christ brings must have ears to listen and pay attention to what Jesus says. Those who listen will continue to gain understanding and truth, but those who do not listen will only sink deeper into the darkness of disbelief and ignorance.

In the next parable, Jesus describes how the kingdom of God is like a growing seed. He presents the example of a man who scatters his seed and experiences the seed's growth without his help. The seed grows into a flourishing crop, seemingly all on its own. Here, Jesus describes God's hand in the building of His kingdom. The ability of the seed to grow without the man's hand reveals how the kingdom of God is not dependent on human effort. Although God in His sovereignty often uses believers to help build His kingdom, it is God who ultimately produces the growth.

Jesus follows up this parable with a similar parable. In verses 30–32, Jesus describes how the kingdom of God can be compared to a small mustard seed. The seed may be small, but when it is sown, it flourishes bigger and taller than all the other plants.

This parable of Jesus reveals the reality of God's kingdom. The kingdom of God is different than we might think. Jesus does not describe the kingdom of God by comparing the kingdom to something grand but to something as small as a seed. This does not mean that the kingdom of God is not powerful, but this does mean the kingdom of God grows by humble means.

God's kingdom is coming no matter what, but the way God's kingdom expands in the present can often be missed. But even though the kingdom of God may seem small and inconspicuous, the kingdom flourishes and expands. One day, God's kingdom will come in its fullness with grandeur and glory, but for now, God's kingdom is spread in ordinary ways, through ordinary people, by the power of God.

Jesus told His disciples how the secret of the kingdom has been revealed to them, and the secret of the kingdom has been revealed to us as well. How? By Jesus giving us eyes and ears to pay attention. The light of Christ has opened our eyes to the truth of the gospel and the workings of God's kingdom. While the world may see grandeur and glory as what defines greatness, we see clearly how true greatness is the small, humble, and seemingly insignificant. The way God's kingdom works does not minimize its greatness—it magnifies its greatness.

These sowing parables connect with the previous parable about the lamp. The light of Christ may seem hidden for the moment, but soon His light will shine brightly. In the same way, God's kingdom may seem hidden for the moment, but one day, the kingdom will come in its fullness and be greater than anyone could ever imagine.

The reality of God's kingdom encourages us as we work for God's kingdom. Our work for the Lord may seem small or insignificant. What we do may go unnoticed or be overlooked by others. And our ministry for the Lord may seem unfruitful at the moment—but there is a harvest of abundance to come. God is working through us to bring others to faith in Christ, causing His kingdom to flourish even if we cannot see the growth just yet. One day, we will see the fruits of our labor, and that makes our labor in the here and now worthwhile.

The light of Christ has opened our eyes to the truth of the gospel and the workings of God's kingdom.

How do believers receive the secret of the kingdom?
How does knowing this secret impact the way we live?

Read 1 Corinthians 3:5—9. Why is it important to remember that God is the One who produces the growth of His kingdom? How does this truth motivate you in your evangelism, or sharing the gospel?

How does the secret of the kingdom encourage you when you feel like your work for the Lord is insignificant?

Jesus has more power than
all the powers of darkness.

Who is This?

READ MARK 4:35–5:43

Watching someone we do not know do something incredible would most likely lead us to say, "Who is this?" In today's passage, the disciples ask the same question. Through a torrential storm, an encounter with a demon-possessed man, and two situations of disease and death, Jesus answers this question, proving that He is the Son of God.

Mark begins by describing the disciples and Jesus on the Sea of Galilee. Jesus is asleep in the boat after a long day of ministry, but His disciples are fighting hard against a horrible storm. The disciples wake Jesus up in alarm and accuse Him of not caring about them in this deadly situation. Immediately Jesus rebukes the wind and the waves, and the once-violent storm becomes still. Jesus turns to His disciples and questions their faith. Why are they afraid when they should trust Him? However, the disciples' response in Mark 4:41 reveals that the disciples were then even more afraid than they were before Jesus calmed the storm. They had watched this man demonstrate immense power by silencing a deadly storm, and they were afraid to be in the presence of such a man. Their fear compels them to ask, "Who then is this?"

Next, Mark tells of an encounter Jesus has with a demon-possessed man. This man is possessed by such powerful demons that no one can restrain or subdue him. But while the demons inside the man are strong, they are not stronger than Jesus. The demons recognize that Jesus is the Son of the Most High God, and they are terrified of what Jesus will do to them. Mark 5:13 says that Jesus gave permission to the demons to enter into a herd of pigs nearby, further demonstrating His power over evil. Agents of darkness have no power over Jesus, and they cannot operate without His permission. This is a comforting reminder to us as we not only battle with sin but live in a world full of sin. Evil may seem to reign, but Jesus reigns over evil. Jesus has more power than all the powers of darkness.

The people's response to Jesus is similar to that of the disciples. They are afraid, but the response of the liberated man is different. This man is so grateful for what Jesus has done for him that he asks Jesus if he could remain with Him. But instead of allowing this man to join Him, Jesus tells the man to proclaim his testimony to his own people, telling them all that God did for him. Unlike the disciples and the people around Jesus, Jesus's actions cause the man to move toward Jesus rather than away.

There is no evidence of fear, only an immense desire to remain close to Jesus.

In the next section, Mark tells of Jesus's interaction with a diseased woman and a dying girl. Jairus, a synagogue leader, falls at Jesus's feet and begs Him to help his little girl. Jairus displays faith in Jesus as he believes that if Jesus lays His hands on his daughter, she will be well. But before Jesus goes to Jairus's house, He stops to interact with a diseased woman. This woman had been suffering from a bleeding disorder for many years, and hearing about Jesus was enough for her to pursue Him for healing. Similar to Jairus, this woman believes that if she could touch Jesus, she would be made well. And sure enough, when she touches Jesus's clothing, her body is instantly healed. Jesus stops and calls for whoever touched Him to come forward, and the woman makes herself known. In response, Jesus publicly proclaims that this woman's faith has made her well. Jesus's response does not mean that it was the woman's faith alone that saved her; it was Jesus's power that ultimately saved her. But it was the woman's faith in Jesus that made her pursue Jesus and receive His grace that made her well.

However, stopping to interact with this woman allowed for more time to progress, and now Jairus's daughter is dead. But Jesus encourages Jairus, telling him to not be afraid, only believe. Jesus comes into Jairus's home and speaks to the girl, commanding her to wake from the dead. Immediately, the girl rises and begins to walk again.

Throughout these several encounters, we repeatedly witness Jesus's power. The situation in the storm displays Jesus's power over creation. The encounter with the demon-possessed man displays Jesus's power of darkness, and the experiences with the diseased woman and dead girl display Jesus's power over disease and death. These happenings whisper of Jesus's actions to come. Soon, Jesus will display His power over darkness and death in a mightier way by dying on the cross and rising from the dead.

All of Jesus's actions answer the disciples' question, "Who then is this?" Jesus is Lord over all creation. But unlike the disciples, who Jesus is should encourage our faith rather than motivate our fear. As believers, we should respond to Jesus's power with holy reverence and awe, but like the liberated man, Jairus, and the woman, we should also respond with trust. Who Jesus is compels us to trust Him. The fact that Jesus is more powerful than anything that seems scary to us encourages us to draw close to Him and trust Him. And even when we struggle to have faith, we can still choose to step forward in trust rather than step away in fear. The disciples failed to do the very thing that we, too, so often fail to do—place our trust in Jesus. When we are afraid, it is not the strength of our faith that matters but the object of our faith. In any and every situation, we can place our trust in Jesus, believing that He will help us even if we do not have all the answers. Jesus is Lord over all things; therefore, we can trust Him with all things.

Jesus is Lord over all things; therefore, we can trust Him with all things.

Day Three — Questions

What keeps you from trusting in Jesus when you are afraid?

How does knowing who Jesus is encourage you to trust Him?

How does Jesus's power to bring liberation and deliverance demonstrate His love for us?

How does His love for us connect to the gospel?

How do you think Jairus felt when Jesus took too long to help his daughter?

How does the end result of that story encourage you to trust Jesus's timing?

Jesus did not allow the people's disbelief to prevent Him from continuing to do His ministry.

Stumbling Blocks of Unbelief

READ MARK 6:1–29

In the previous passage, we learned of several people's faith in Jesus. However, in today's passage, we learn that not everyone believed and trusted in Jesus. The people in today's passages are marked by unbelief and teach us the reality of hardened hearts to the gospel. While this unbelief is disappointing, Jesus perseveres in His ministry, teaching us as believers to endure rejection, ridicule, and persecution so that the gospel is heard and known.

Chapter 6 opens with Jesus returning to His hometown to teach. We would think that the people in Jesus's hometown would accept Him, but instead, He is rejected. The people who gathered to watch Jesus teach were astonished by His authority. They were amazed how this uneducated man could know so much about Scripture and teach the truths of Scripture with such wisdom and authority. However, this astonishment did not equate with belief. The people's amazement causes them to question Jesus's credibility. They question how this man could have power and wisdom when He was the son of a carpenter and a woman rumored to have birthed Jesus out of wedlock. The questions of these people reveal how the people did not believe that Jesus could be a man and also the Son of God.

The people in Nazareth are not only astonished by Jesus; they are also offended by Him. The root of the Greek word for "offense" in this verse means "stumbling block." This word is often used by Mark to describe obstructions that prevent people from following Jesus and having faith in Him. This idea of a stumbling block is reflected in 1 Peter 2:7–8 when Peter says, "The stone that the builders rejected—this one has become the cornerstone, and a stone to stumble over, and a rock to trip over." The people's unbelief was a stumbling block that prevented them from knowing Jesus and receiving His salvation. They have rejected Jesus, the cornerstone of the gospel message, and therefore, they rejected the salvation He offers.

Jesus responds to the people in two ways. First, He responds by saying, "A prophet is not without honor except in his hometown, among his relatives, and in his household" (Mark 6:4). Through this proverbial phrase, Jesus reveals how just as a prophet is rejected by those closest to him, so is Jesus rejected by those closest to Him. Second, Jesus responds with amazement at the people's lack of faith. Jesus is not amazed by the sin of the people, but He is amazed by their hard hearts and refusal to believe in

Him. These people had seen and heard of Jesus's teaching and healings, but these things were not enough for them. To them, Jesus was an ordinary man, and their focus on the ordinary led them to miss the extraordinary. Their focus on His humanity caused them to miss His divinity. The response of these people shows how one can know who Jesus is and be acquainted with His works and teachings but still not believe in Him.

We also see an example of disbelief in Mark 6:14–20. Through this account of Herod, we learn how Herod was interested in Jesus and the teachings of John, yet his interest did not lead to belief. Herod was curious about John's teaching about Jesus, and he liked to listen to John's words, but Herod did not believe the words John spoke. Herod is an example of a person who is attracted to the message of Christianity and is curious about Jesus, but their curiosity and interest do not move forward in belief. Herod doubts that Jesus is the Son of God and only assumes that Jesus's power comes from John being resurrected from the dead. Those around Herod also doubt Jesus's divinity, and they assume that Jesus is a prophet.

Both the response of the people in Nazareth and the response of Herod show us the reality of unbelief. In today's world, we can see how people create stumbling blocks for themselves that prevent them from believing in Jesus. There are people all around us, with hearts hardened to the gospel, who cannot believe that a man from Nazareth could also be the Son of God. Like the people in this passage, they may believe that Jesus was a good moral teacher or a prophet, but they fail to believe He was

God in the flesh. It is sad to see how exposure to the gospel does not always mean belief in the gospel. The good news of salvation through Jesus is too often rejected because of disbelief—disbelief that one needs Jesus for salvation, disbelief that Jesus is who He says He is, and disbelief that Jesus could be both human and God.

Like Jesus, as believers, we are often amazed by people's hardened hearts. But although this disbelief can be upsetting to us, we are still called as believers to spread the message of the gospel. Tucked in between these two passages of disbelief, we read an account of Jesus commissioning His disciples to preach and heal the sick. Jesus did not allow the people's disbelief to prevent Him from continuing to do His ministry beyond Nazareth. He gave authority to His disciples to continue to make the gospel known, and He gives believers the same authority (Matthew 28:16–20).

While rejection, ridicule, and persecution can be painful, as followers of Christ, we must persevere. We can be encouraged by reminding ourselves how God has the power to remove the stumbling blocks of disbelief. God's pursuing grace can transform even the hardest of hearts. Knowing that God can and does work through disbelief encourages us to share the gospel. And because we know the Holy Spirit works through us to soften hearts that are hardened to the gospel's message, we need to share the gospel's message. We do not have to allow disbelief to discourage us, but rather, we can allow it to motivate us to continue making the gospel known. Jesus did not give up, and neither should we.

God's pursuing grace can transform even the hardest of hearts.

Day Four — Questions

John the Baptist remained dedicated to preaching the truth, even though it led to his death. How does John the Baptist encourage you to remain dedicated to the gospel, even in persecution?

What are some ways that you see people create stumbling blocks for themselves when it comes to belief in the gospel?

How can you trust that God can still work through hardened hearts when people you know reject the gospel? Write down the names of the people you know who reject the gospel, and pray for God to remove the stumbling blocks of their disbelief.

God provides even when
our situation seems hopeless.

Abundance in the Wilderness

There are moments in our lives when provision seems slim. Whether the money in your bank account has dwindled or you keep receiving a "no" for different job opportunities, it can be hard to trust that God will come through. In today's passage, Jesus performs His most public miracle yet to show how God has the ability to bring forth abundance in the wilderness. Through this miracle, Jesus not only demonstrates His power but teaches those present, as well as us today, how God provides even when our situation seems hopeless.

Today's passage opens with the disciples bringing back a report to Jesus. The disciples had just come back from successful ministry endeavors, and they were excited to tell Jesus all they had done. While Jesus recognizes their efforts, He encourages them to take some time to rest. Jesus and His disciples travel to a remote place to rest but are followed by a large group of people. Most of us would likely become frustrated to lose our moment of rest, but not Jesus. He looks upon the group of people with compassion. The root of the Greek word for "compassion" means to have your bowels moved. This is because during the time this was written, people believed that love and pity came from the bowels. Thus, this means that Jesus's care for this group of people was not a surface-level concern but a deep level of compassion and love. Mark writes that Jesus's compassion was fueled by the fact that the group of people was like sheep without a shepherd. Like a helpless and lost flock of sheep, these people needed direction. They needed to be guided to the truth, and Jesus sees their spiritual need as a greater priority than His need to rest.

By stopping to teach these people, Jesus placed Himself as the shepherd of the lost flock. This imagery runs deep. In Numbers 27:15–17, Moses asked God, "May the Lord, the God who gives breath to all, appoint a man over the community who will go out before them and come back in before them, and who will bring them out and bring them in, so that the Lord's community won't be like sheep without a shepherd." Like the crowd before Jesus, the Israelites needed a leader who would guide and shepherd them after Moses died. God was faithful to raise up another leader for Israel, but Scripture also points to an ultimate leader to come. In Ezekiel 34, God promises He will establish a shepherd over Israel who will provide, help, and care for His people. Jesus is this promised shepherd, the Good Shepherd, who God has appointed to save His sheep. The compassion we see from Jesus in this passage reflects Jesus's love for His people, a love so deep that He was willing to lay down His life for them (John 10:11).

As Jesus teaches, the light begins to fade, and the disciples encourage Jesus to let the people go. They were in a desolate place, a wilderness essentially, and there was no food to be found in the wilderness. The disciples believe that Jesus should send them away to another area to find food, but Jesus has other plans. He tells the disciples that they are the ones who should provide food for the people. However, there was a problem—two problems, to be exact. The group of people was so large that it would take about two hundred denarii—a significant amount of money the disciples did not have—to feed them. Their financial situation would prove hopeless, but so would their material situation. The disciples only had five loaves and two fish. With little money and little food, the disciples found themselves in an unlikely situation for provision.

Jesus organizes the group into smaller groups, prays to the Lord, and begins passing out the bread and fish. One by one, each person receives enough food to eat and be satisfied. Mark also specifies that there was enough left over to fill twelve baskets, enough for each disciple to be satisfied, as well. Christ's ability to feed over five thousand people reflects the actions of God in Exodus 16 when God provided food for the Israelites in the wilderness. Through Jesus's miracle, those present were able to witness how God has the power to bring life from a place of death. Ultimately, God's ability to bring life from death points us to Jesus. Though Jesus died on the cross and was placed in a tomb, the power of God raised Him to new life. Even in a place of death, God has the power to bring forth life.

By His grace, this is what God does for us as well. In John 6, Jesus proclaims that He is the Bread of Life, meaning that He is the one true source of life. By dying on the cross, Jesus has given us His grace that covers our sin and gives us eternal life. His grace has also given us new life by causing our old sinful selves to die, giving us a new self that has the ability to fight sin through the help of the Spirit.

While Jesus has met our ultimate spiritual need through His death and resurrection, He also meets our daily spiritual needs. He gives us grace and forgiveness when we sin, peace for our fears, and strength when we face trials and temptations. All our spiritual needs are met in Christ. And because of this, we can trust that our physical needs will be met by Jesus, too. As God's sheep, we can always trust our Good Shepherd to provide for us, even when our situation seems hopeless. He may not always provide in the ways we expect, but we can always count on Him to give us what we need. We serve a God who brings life from death and abundance in the wilderness, so let us trust Him.

We serve a God who brings life from death and abundance in the wilderness, so let us trust Him.

Day Five — Questions

What does Jesus being the Good Shepherd reveal about His character?

How does Jesus's ability to provide, even in an unlikely situation, encourage you to trust Him in moments when provision seems hopeless?

List out some of your spiritual and physical needs. Spend some time in prayer, asking for God's provision and asking God to help you trust His provision.

When Jesus overheard what was said,

he told the synagogue leader,

"Don't be afraid. Only believe."

MARK 5:36

Week Two — Reflection

Summarize the main points from this week's Scripture readings.

What did you observe from this week's passages about God and His character?

What do this week's passages reveal about the condition of mankind and yourself?

How do these passages point to the gospel?

How should you respond to these passages? What specific action steps can you take this week to apply them in your life?

Write a prayer in response to your study of God's Word. Adore God for who He is, confess sins He revealed in your own life, ask Him to empower you to walk in obedience, and pray for anyone who comes to mind as you study.

By God's grace. He broke through
our hardened hearts with
the truth of the gospel.

It is I

READ MARK 6:45–56

The disciples had just witnessed Jesus perform an incredible miracle. They had seen their teacher feed thousands of people by multiplying five loaves and two fish. We would imagine that such a miracle would cause the disciples' faith in Jesus to deepen, but unfortunately, that is not the case. In today's passage, we learn that the disciples have a ways to go before their belief in Jesus is strong, but even though their faith is small, Jesus continues to teach them who He is. Through another miraculous encounter on the sea, Jesus demonstrates to His disciples not only His identity as God but the glory of God.

After feeding the five thousand, Jesus sends His disciples into a boat to leave. Jesus stays behind to say goodbye to the crowd and go up to a mountain to pray. Jesus must have prayed for a while because now it is nighttime, and the disciples' boat is in the middle of the sea. The disciples are facing a strong wind, and they are struggling to maintain control of their boat because of the storm. Jesus sees their struggle and comes to His disciples. However, Jesus's mode of going to His disciples is unique. Jesus does not swim out to His disciples or take a boat of His own. He walks on water. Yet Jesus's choice to walk on water is not a haphazard decision but an intentional display of His identity. By walking on water, Jesus displays four examples of His identity as the Son of God.

First, the fact that Jesus is walking on water reveals how He is the Son of God. The disciples have already seen Jesus's power over creation in their first storm on the sea, and now they see His power over creation in this miraculous way. The same One who calmed the waves is the same One walking on the waves. The disciples believe that Jesus is a ghost because no one has the ability to walk on water. But Jesus is not an ordinary man; He is God in the flesh. Only God has the power to walk on water.

Second, Mark gives a detail that may seem minuscule to us but is rather powerful. In verse 48, Mark says that Jesus wanted to pass by the disciples' boat. This language of "passing" reflects an Old Testament encounter Moses had with God. In Exodus 33:18–23, Moses asked God to show him His glory. God told Moses that Moses could not see His face, for no one can look upon God fully without dying. Instead, God placed Moses in a crevice of a rock and covered his face. Only after God passed by Moses could Moses look upon God, but he could only look at God's back. This encounter between Moses and God is an example of a theophany, which is an appearance and manifestation of

God. Like this Old Testament encounter, Jesus is manifesting the glory of God to His disciples. Just as God passed by Moses to show him His glory, perhaps Jesus planned to pass by His disciples to show them His glory.

Third, Jesus not only shows He is the Son of God; He also declares He is the Son of God. Seeing the disciples' fear, Jesus calls out, "It is I. Don't be afraid" (verse 50). The phrase "It is I" is the Greek translation of God's words of "I Am" to Moses in Exodus 3:14. God used the words "I AM" to declare His identity to Moses. Jesus uses the same words to declare His deity and equality with the Father. The Great I AM displayed His glory to the Israelites by parting the sea, and Jesus, the Great I AM, displays His glory to His disciples by walking on the sea.

Lastly, as Jesus comes into the boat, the winds cease. Once again, Jesus demonstrates His power and glory to His disciples by calming another storm. But even though Jesus has manifested His glory in several ways, the disciples do not believe. Mark tells us that they were completely astounded because they did not understand the miracle of the loaves and fish. The disciples' hearts were hardened, meaning that even a miracle in the wilderness and a miracle on the sea would not be enough to make them believe. Again, Mark shows us how simply knowing about Jesus and witnessing His miracles does not mean instant faith. It will take time for the disciples' hearts to soften and their faith to deepen, but Jesus remains patient through this process.

Unlike the hardened hearts of the disciples, those of us in Christ have our hearts softened because of God's grace. Because of sin, our hearts were once hardened to the truth of the gospel, but the same God who said, "'Let light shine out of darkness,' has shone in our hearts to give the light of the knowledge of God's glory in the face of Jesus Christ" (2 Corinthians 4:6). By God's grace, He broke through our hardened hearts with the truth of the gospel, declaring His glory in the face of Jesus. As believers, we are witnesses to the glory of God because we have experienced His glory through the forgiveness of Jesus Christ.

Just like Jesus's first miracle on the sea, Jesus's display of glory in this passage encourages us to trust Him. Like the disciples, we can encounter storms of temptation, trials, and troubles, and we can lose sight of who Jesus is in the midst of those storms. But in these situations, we must remember who Jesus is. We must remember that Jesus is the Great I AM who is more powerful than anything on earth. Only He is able to calm the storms we face in our lives, but we must place our trust in Him over and over again. In every moment of fear, Jesus says to us, "Have courage! It is I. Don't be afraid."

In every moment of fear, Jesus says to us, "Have courage! It is I. Don't be afraid."

Day One — Questions

Is there a current situation you are facing that is making it difficult to trust Jesus? How can it help you in this situation to remind yourself of who Jesus is?

What does Jesus's patience, even in His disciples' unbelief, say about His character? What does this mean for you when you wrestle with unbelief?

How does Jesus's patience with His disciples encourage our patience in evangelism and discipleship?

There is nothing we could do to
make our sinful hearts clean:
it is all through Christ's grace alone.

True Purification

The Pharisees in Jesus's time were known for their religious piety. They boasted of their obedience to the Scriptures and looked down on anyone who failed to keep the Law and Jewish traditions. In today's passage, the Pharisees confront Jesus for the actions of His disciples, but it is through this interaction that Jesus exposes not only the Pharisees' misguided thinking but also their sinful hearts. The Pharisees believed that their behavior made them clean, but Jesus reveals the source of true purification.

The Pharisees observe the disciples eating with unclean hands, and they are aghast. They ask Jesus why His disciples refuse to keep the tradition of the elders by not washing their hands. It was a tradition for Jews to ceremonially wash their hands throughout the day to rid themselves of anything unclean. This tradition was more about holiness than hygiene. The tradition of the elders, as drawn from the Law, emphasized that a person must not touch anything unclean, including a dead body, a sick body, or any bodily fluid. Any kind of uncleanliness was equated with the defilement of purity and holiness.

Jesus calls the Pharisees hypocrites and quotes a passage from Isaiah that shows their hypocrisy. The Pharisees may honor God with their lips, but their hearts are actually far from Him (Isaiah 29:13). Their worship is not true worship because their hearts are not seeking to be obedient to the Lord. Instead of putting God's Word first, they put human tradition first, revealing that they care more about what man says than what God says.

Jesus continues by saying that by holding on to human tradition, they abandon God's commandments. By following their own traditions, they make loopholes in Scripture that keep them from obeying God's Word. In doing so, they invalidate and nullify God's Word, meaning they make God's Word obsolete by replacing God's commands with traditions. Sadly, people can do the same thing today, often without realizing they are doing so. People can believe that good works, cultural traditions, or church rituals make them holy and blameless before God. And while traditions can encourage our holiness, traditions do not define our holiness. God's Word shapes our holiness and must be placed first above tradition. Human traditions do not and should not take the place of God's Word.

Jesus goes deeper by revealing what truly defiles a person. He says that it is not what is on the outside that defiles a person but what is on the inside (verse 15). The Pharisees believed that touching anything unclean or doing anything that was against tradition defiled a person, but Jesus refutes their thinking. His emphasis on the inside teaches that it is the human heart that makes one unclean. The human heart is wicked and sinful, and nothing we can do on the outside can make our hearts clean. The Pharisees ignored what was within by focusing on outward piety. In doing so, they are the ones who are truly unclean. Their prideful hearts and hypocritical lips proved that their hearts were far from God and desperately sinful.

It may seem that this passage does not give us the answer to what makes our hearts clean. However, Mark adds an editorial note that gives us the answer. In verse 19, Mark says that Jesus declared all foods clean. This small note holds immense truth. By saying this, Jesus reveals how He has come to bring purification. Jesus has come to declare sinners clean by washing them with His own blood. Therefore ritual cleansing and other traditions have not been nullified but fulfilled through Christ. Those things are not needed to be pure in God's eyes—a pure and redeemed heart is what matters, given to us by Jesus alone. With His grace and forgiveness, Jesus cleanses our unclean hearts, giving us pure and renewed hearts. There is nothing we could do to make our sinful hearts clean; it is all through Christ's grace alone. Second Corinthians 5:21 says, "He made the one who did not know sin to be sin for us, so that in him we might become the righteousness of God." Jesus was defiled so that we could be clean.

Only Jesus can purify us from the inside out. Even those of us who have walked with Jesus for a while can benefit from remembering this truth. Sometimes we can fall into the mentality that what we do makes us holy and righteous in God's eyes. We can think that we must do all of the spiritual disciplines perfectly, have perfect church attendance on Sunday mornings, or take as many volunteer opportunities as we can to find acceptance and favor with God. However, the gospel declares that it is not what we do but what Christ has done that determines our acceptance with God. We obey God and live a life of holiness and faithfulness out of a response to the gospel, for it is Christ's grace alone that makes our hearts pure.

While Jesus has made our hearts pure, we can respond to His grace by continuing to walk in holiness. We can do this in two ways. The first is by having a continual heart of repentance. In verses 21–22, Jesus lists the sins that flow out of a sinful heart. While Christ has given us redeemed hearts, we still have a sin nature, and we will struggle to always walk in holiness. We should notice what comes out of us—sins like pride, anger, or slander—and confess our sins to the Lord. As we repent, we rest in the Spirit's power to help us walk in holiness. Remaining rooted in God's Word also keeps our motivations and actions pure. We walk in holiness as we obey God's Word and keep God's Word a priority in our lives.

There is freedom in knowing we do not have to do anything to make our hearts pure. We can surrender our attempts to earn righteousness and rest in what Christ has done.

We can surrender our attempts to earn righteousness and rest in what Christ has done.

Day Two — Questions

In what ways do you struggle with doing good works, rituals, or traditions to please God and earn His favor?

How can you rest in Christ's grace when you find your obedience falling short?

Take a moment to examine your heart. Is there anything sinful flowing out of it that you need to confess? Spend some time in repentance over the sins the Spirit reveals.

In His love, goodness, and mercy,
Christ chose to sacrifice Himself
so that our sins could be forgiven.

Eyes to See & Ears to Hear

MARK 7:24–8:26

Throughout our study of Mark so far, we have repeatedly seen the themes of insiders versus outsiders and belief versus unbelief. In today's passages, we see both of those themes present as Jesus interacts with a Gentile woman, heals two men, and interacts once again with the Pharisees. By these interactions and themes, we continue to learn the beauty of simple trust in Jesus Christ.

The first interaction Jesus has is with a Gentile woman. Gentiles were non-Jewish people, and because they did not belong to the people of Israel, they were deemed unclean by Jews. Despite her status, this woman comes to Jesus and boldly asks for healing. Jesus's response to this woman appears rude on the surface, but Jesus is not speaking with words of unkindness. In fact, Jesus is testing this woman by using a parable to see what her response would be to His words. Jesus uses this parable to describe how He has come to speak His message of salvation primarily to the people of Israel. While we will see later on in Scripture how the gospel is for both Jew and Gentile, Jesus's priority was to speak to the people of Israel first, to reveal how He is the fulfillment of the promised Messiah, as well as the fulfillment of all the Hebrew Scriptures and traditions.

The woman not only understands Jesus's parable, but she responds accordingly. She tells Jesus that she may not be among the people of Israel, but she is in need of Jesus's salvation and healing just as much as the Israelites. Just as a household pet eats the crumbs that fall off the dinner table, this woman has come to receive a morsel of blessing from Jesus. Jesus is impressed by her response, and in Matthew 15:28, we learn of Jesus's reply to the woman as He says, "Woman, your faith is great." The woman's interaction with Jesus reveals how, unlike those with hardened hearts to Jesus's words, this woman listens and understands His words. And more than that, she responds to Jesus's words as a demonstration of her faith, revealing that she believes who Jesus is, and she desires to receive what only He could give, even though she is undeserving of Jesus's grace.

This short interaction with Jesus reveals the gospel. Like the Gentile woman, we are all undeserving of Christ's grace. We are all sinful, unclean people who do not have a place at the Master's table. But in His love, goodness, and mercy, Christ chose to sacrifice Himself so that our sins could be forgiven. He became like a dog—lowly and outcast—so we could be exalted and given a place at His table. Those of us in Christ have been given a seat at God's table, even though we did not deserve such a position, all because of the grace of Jesus.

After this interaction, Jesus goes on to perform three more miracles. He heals a deaf man, restores sight to a blind man, and feeds a crowd of four thousand people. Once again, Jesus demonstrates the compassion of God by His healings, and He provides a large crowd with the means to eat. Jesus then encounters the Pharisees, who seek to test Jesus's authority by asking Him to perform a sign. This request from the Pharisees demonstrates their hardened hearts. If they believed in who Jesus was, they would not need a sign from Him. Jesus's response is to sigh deeply in His spirit—a reflection of His grief over the Pharisees' unbelieving hearts—and refuse to give the Pharisees a sign.

Jesus's interaction with the Pharisees causes Him to warn His disciples to beware of the leaven of the Pharisees. Jesus uses figurative language to explain that just as a small amount of yeast spreads and controls a whole batch of bread dough, so has the unbelief of the Pharisees spread and taken control of their hearts. Jesus warns the disciples not to let their own unbelief spread and multiply within their hearts. However, through Jesus's discussion with His disciples, we see how the disciples are still struggling with their faith. Even after the miracle of the four thousand, the disciples question how they are going to have enough food to eat. Jesus hears their words and questions their unbelief.

Jesus's question in Mark 8:18, in which He asks, "Do you have eyes and not see; do you have ears and not hear?" is significant in light of the two miracles Jesus performs in this passage. Jesus heals a deaf man and a blind man, two people who once could not see and could not hear. But this miracle of physical blindness and deafness speaks to the hardened hearts of those who do not believe in Jesus. By refusing to believe who Jesus is or to take in the words He speaks, they are spiritually blind and deaf. The disciples, too, are experiencing spiritual blindness and deafness as their faith in Jesus is still growing. But Jesus's inclusion of the word "yet" in verse 21 reveals Jesus's understanding that their faith will grow and their hearts will soften, even if it takes time.

Those of us in Christ may have had our ears and eyes opened to the message of the gospel, but we can still struggle with unbelief. Jesus's warning to the disciples is a warning for us as well—it is a warning to keep unbelief from spreading within us. As believers, there will be times when doubt arises, when we struggle to believe who God is or what His Word says. Even though these doubts are normal, we should be careful not to let unbelief spread by closing our eyes and ears to God's Word or refusing to be in community with other believers. We need God's Word and other believers to remind us over and over again who Jesus is. The seed of unbelief can be kept from flourishing as we remain close to God and His Word.

Those of us in Christ have been given a seat at God's table.

Day Three — Questions

What does Jesus's desire to help someone who is considered an outsider reveal about His character? What does this mean for you?

How are you tempted to rely on a display of God's power to believe in Him? How can you trust who He is without needing to see visible evidence of His power?

Why is it important to go to God's Word in moments of unbelief?

Following Jesus comes with a cost,
but the cost is always worth it.

Take Up Your Cross

READ MARK 8:27–9:1

Jesus's disciples have shown slow progress in their belief in Jesus, but in today's passage, we see how their faith has grown. Through a public confession, Jesus's disciples proclaim Christ's identity as the Son of God. Through this confession, as well as further teaching from Jesus, we learn what it truly looks like to know and follow Jesus.

Jesus is walking with His disciples when He asks them two questions. First, He asks, "Who do people say I am?" They respond that people say He is John the Baptist, Elijah, or another prophet. But then Jesus asks another question in light of these claims, "Who do you say that I am?" It is one thing for the disciples to recognize what others believe about Jesus, but it is another for the disciples to recognize who they believe Jesus to be.

This should be something that we consider in our own lives. Many people will make claims about who Jesus is. Some will say that He was a good man, a moral teacher, or a prophet. But who do we believe Jesus is? We should be quick to not believe the claims of others without stopping to think about what we believe about Jesus ourselves. We should not look to the claims of others but to the truth of Scripture to help guide our understanding of who Jesus is.

Peter's response to Jesus's question is the one and only true response: Jesus is the Messiah. The word "Messiah," or "Christ," means "Anointed One." Throughout the Old Testament, God spoke to the prophets of an Anointed King who would come to save God's people and bring justice and restoration. Peter's public confession reveals his understanding that Jesus is the fulfillment of the promised Anointed One. Jesus is the Messiah.

But things take a turn when Jesus reveals God's plan to His disciples. Jesus tells His disciples that the Son of Man will be rejected and killed, but He will rise again three days later. Jesus's title of Son of Man for Himself comes from Daniel 7, in which a promised Son of Man will arise to bring restoration upon the earth. Jesus is the promised Son of Man who will bring restoration to people, but He will do it in an unexpected way.

Peter is taken aback by Jesus's words and rebukes Jesus for His words. Peter, as well as so many other Jews, expected the Son of Man—the Anointed One—to bring reform and restoration in a mighty way. They expected the Messiah to overthrow the government, not for the government to overthrow Him. But Jesus rebukes Peter in return, saying that Peter is concerned with a human agenda rather than God's plan.

Jesus then goes on to teach about what it truly means to follow Him. He presents three aspects of discipleship: deny yourself, take up your cross, and follow me. To deny oneself is a change of allegiance that shifts from following one's sinful desires to following God and His ways. To be a follower of Jesus, we must repent and turn away from our sin. We must recognize that we deserve punishment for our sin, but through Christ's grace, we receive forgiveness.

Next, we are to take up our cross. As we will read shortly, Jesus takes up a physical cross to give us salvation, and as believers, we are called to spiritually take up our own cross. The cross is a symbol of sacrifice, and the life of discipleship is a continual sacrifice. Following Jesus comes with a cost, but the cost is always worth it. Following Jesus will cost us our reputation, our plans, and our desires. While it is painful to take up one's cross, doing so leads to true life. Our salvation cost Jesus a painful death on the cross, but it led to life for all who believe in Him. As we embrace the cost of following Jesus with joyful and grateful hearts, we experience the life that has been given to us through Christ. This is why Jesus goes on to say in verse 35 that to gain life, one must lose their life. For us to follow Jesus, there needs to be a death to our old selves. But when we die to our old, sinful selves, we are able to live as the people we were created to be. We are our truest selves when we walk in the newness of life Jesus provides.

Lastly, we are to follow Jesus. Jesus says in verse 36 that it does nothing to gain the world but lose one's life. In other words, pursuing the fleeting desires of this world or receiving the approval of man does not lead to life—it leads to death. Fame, riches, status, and so many other things that this world upholds do not and cannot give us true and lasting life. In order to follow Jesus, we must remove our attachment to this world. We must turn away from what we are trying to pursue as the means for identity and purpose. Our identity and purpose are found in Christ alone, so we must follow Christ alone.

In Luke's account of this passage, he records Jesus saying that we are to daily take up our cross (Luke 9:23). Our sinful flesh will tempt us to follow our own desires or the things of this world. But through the power of the Spirit, we are given the strength to daily put ourselves to death by choosing to follow Jesus instead of the desires of the flesh. Daily, we are to choose to follow Jesus, even when life is hard or walking in holiness is a struggle. Daily, we are to choose to see Jesus as better than the things of this world, choosing to die to our own agenda to pursue God's ways and plans. Following Jesus is a day-to-day response, but it yields an eternity of true and lasting life.

> Our identity and purpose are found in Christ alone, so we must follow Christ alone.

Day Four — Questions

In verse 31, Jesus says that it is necessary for the Son of Man to die. Look up Ephesians 2:1—9. Why was it necessary for Jesus to die?

What is keeping you from following Jesus more faithfully? How can you turn from those things to pursue obedience to Christ?

Which of the three aspects of discipleship (denying yourself, taking up your cross, following Him) are you struggling the most with right now? Spend some time in prayer, asking for God's help in this area and for the Spirit's strength to help you be faithful to God in this area.

Through Jesus, we have full and complete
access to the presence of God.

Jesus Transfigured

READ MARK 9:2–13

Jesus has repeatedly shown His disciples His deity and authority as the Son of God, but in today's passage, Jesus displays His deity in a way He has not done thus far. Jesus takes three disciples up to a mountain and allows them to witness face-to-face the fullness of God's glory.

In verse 2, Mark tells us how Jesus was transfigured before the disciples. The word "transfigured" means "to be transformed in form," like a caterpillar transformed into a butterfly. Jesus still maintains His humanity, but His divinity is no longer veiled. In Luke's account, Luke describes how Jesus's face changed (Luke 9:29), but Mark focuses on Jesus's clothes, revealing how His garments became dazzling white. Jesus's clothes reflect His perfect righteousness and purity, and His face reflects the face of Moses, whose face shined bright after witnessing the glory of God. However, Jesus is not reflecting the glory of God but emanating the glory of God as He is God in the flesh.

This amazing encounter continues as Elijah and Moses appear next to Jesus. Mark tells us that the three disciples were terrified, and it is Peter who speaks up, even though he is unsure what to say. Peter suggests they build three shelters to cover Jesus, Elijah, and Moses. The word for "shelter" in this verse means "tabernacle." In the Old Testament, the tabernacle was a shelter, a place of worship for God's presence to dwell with His people. Yet the fullness of His glory was veiled, for the people could not be in the presence of God without perishing.

Peter's suggestion reveals his awareness that he is witnessing the fullness of God's glory, and he attempts to shelter God's glory for fear of death. But instead of God's glory being veiled, God's glory only expands as a cloud covers the mountain, and the voice of God booms, declaring that Jesus is His Son. For a second time, the voice of God confirms Jesus's identity as the Son of God. However, this time God includes a command to listen to Jesus. This encounter on the mountain, including the enveloping cloud, mirrors Moses's encounter with God on Mount Sinai. Moses also witnessed God's glory, but this time, God was allowing the disciples to witness His glory fully with no consequence of death.

Jesus's transfiguration accomplishes several things. First, the transfiguration confirms Peter's confession. In the previous chapter, Peter confesses that Jesus was the Messiah, the Son of God. Here, Peter's confession is confirmed as Jesus reveals the fullness of

His deity as God in the flesh. Second, the transfiguration affirms how Jesus is the fulfillment of the Old Testament. In this passage, Moses represents the Law, and Elijah represents the prophets. Both the Law and prophets pointed to the need for a Savior, but neither could provide salvation. By His death and resurrection, Jesus fulfills the Old Testament by living a sinless life and sacrificing Himself to provide salvation for sinners.

Lastly, Jesus's transfiguration invites the disciples to worship. The presence of God among the people of Israel in the tabernacle gave the people the opportunity to witness God's glory and worship Him. The same is happening for the disciples through Jesus's transfiguration. Yet the disciples are invited to experience the fullness of God in a way never before possible. Jesus was inviting the disciples into the full presence of God, revealing how He is the One who makes access to God possible. Both Moses and Elijah were mouthpieces for God, but they could not bridge the gap between sinful man and Holy God. However, Jesus provides the disciples with a preview of what would soon be available for all those who trust and believe in Him. Through His death and resurrection, Jesus would make it possible for mankind to be brought near to the presence of God with no fear of death. Through Jesus, we have full and complete access to the presence of God.

Jesus commands the disciples not to tell others about this encounter until after His death and resurrection. As they come down the mountain, the disciples ask a question about Elijah. In the book of Malachi, it was prophesied that the Day of the Lord, the day of God's divine judgment and restoration, would come when Elijah appeared (Malachi 4:5). Now that they have seen Elijah on the mountain, the disciples question why Jesus is speaking about His death if the day of God's restoration was near. But Jesus reveals that John the Baptist fulfilled the coming of Elijah, and just as Elijah was rejected and killed, so will Jesus be rejected and killed. It is through Jesus, not Elijah or John the Baptist, that restoration will be made possible.

The three disciples witnessed a worshipful experience on the mountain, but will their belief remain strong after coming off the mountaintop? Soon the disciples will experience a time of trial when Jesus is arrested, which will test whether their faith in Jesus will waver in the midst of hardship. In the same way, as believers, there are times in our own lives when we have "mountaintop" experiences. This can be an emotional high at an event or a church service, or it can even be a pivotal moment when we feel God's presence powerfully. These are incredible, worshipful experiences. But when we return back to the day-to-day and when trials come, the emotion of that experience can fade.

As believers, our worship of Jesus is not dependent on mountaintop experiences. We do not live out our faith and relationship with God from mountaintop to mountaintop but from moment to moment. Even when we feel like we are in the valley, our faith and worship to the Lord can remain strong as we remember who Jesus is and what He has done for us. Jesus remains the same on both the mountaintop and in the valley. Therefore, we can worship Him whether we are on the mountaintop or in the valley.

Jesus remains the same on both the mountaintop and in the valley.

Day Five — Questions

What does it say about God's character that He wants to reveal Himself to us?

How does your full access to God through Jesus impact your day-to-day life?

How can you continue to worship God whether you are on the mountaintop or in the valley?

"If anyone wants to follow after me,
let him deny himself, take up his cross,
and follow me. For whoever wants to
save his life will lose it, but whoever
loses his life because of me and
the gospel will save it."

MARK 8:34B–35

Week Three — Reflection

Summarize the main points from this week's Scripture readings.

What did you observe from this week's passages about God and His character?

What do this week's passages reveal about the condition of mankind and yourself?

How do these passages point to the gospel?

How should you respond to these passages? What specific action steps can you take this week to apply them in your life?

Write a prayer in response to your study of God's Word. Adore God for who He is, confess sins He revealed in your own life, ask Him to empower you to walk in obedience, and pray for anyone who comes to mind as you study.

Jesus calls us to come to Him
with our imperfect faith
and rest in His perfect grace.

I Believe; Help My Unbelief

READ MARK 9:14–29

We all have moments as believers when we waver in our faith—when doubts arise, and our trust in God falters. It can be easy to become frustrated or ashamed of ourselves when we struggle in our faith. But what does Jesus say about moments of unbelief, and what is His response to us? In today's passage, we learn what our response should be when our faith is weak and how Jesus's response to us encourages us in our doubt.

Peter, James, and John had been with Jesus on the mountain, but the rest of the disciples were in the valley. As Jesus and the three disciples meet back with the remaining disciples, they witness a crowd of people and an argument occurring. The disciples had failed to heal a boy who was tormented by a demon, and they were most likely arguing with the scribes about their failure. The father of the boy tells Jesus how the disciples were unable to help his son. Yet again, the disciples show evidence of unbelief.

The disciples had been successful in healing and driving out demons before, so what changed? Later on in the passage, we learn how the disciples failed because they did not pray. The disciples chose to rely on their strength instead of relying on God's strength through prayer. They underestimated the power of spiritual darkness and believed they had enough power in and of themselves to overcome the demon.

Through the disciples' failure, we learn the necessity and power of prayer. As believers, we do not live as independent people, for we are fully dependent on God. We need to come to God in prayer and ask Him to help us by working and moving through the situations of our lives. Coming to God in prayer is an act of dependency. Prayer keeps us from trying to rely on ourselves for strength, and instead, it allows us to rely on the strength of the Lord. We are helpless without the Lord, so we need to come to Him in prayer.

As Jesus interacts with the father of the boy, we learn another example of prayer. The boy's father asks Jesus to heal his son if He can. Jesus responds, "'If you can'? Everything is possible for the one who believes" (verse 23). The father's words to Jesus reveal that though his faith was small, he still believed Jesus was able to help. Recognizing his own lack of faith, the father responds, "I do believe; help my unbelief!" (verse 24). There are two lessons we can learn from both Jesus and the father's response.

Through Jesus's response, we learn how God is willing and able to do the impossible. God is an all-powerful God who acts in mighty and incredible ways. Jesus's response of "If you can?" reveals that there is not one situation in which God fails to work. Because of who God is, all things are possible for God. However, while God can do the impossible, this does not mean that He will always do the impossible. There are moments in God's sovereignty that He chooses not to answer prayer, not because He is not good but because He has other plans. We can still pray for God to do the impossible and trust that God is good, even if the impossible does not happen.

Through the father's response, we learn how we can come to Jesus, even in our moments of unbelief. This man recognized that he was struggling to fully trust God and asked Jesus to help him in his unbelief. The father's response encourages us to come to Jesus with the same prayer in moments of doubt. Instead of allowing unbelief to move us away from Jesus, unbelief can propel us toward Jesus. Instead of allowing unbelief to make us feel ashamed or guilty, we can see unbelief as an opportunity to rest in Christ's grace, knowing that God does not chastise us for our unbelief but wants to help us in and through our unbelief.

This man's response and Jesus's healing of the boy reveal how we do not need to have perfect faith to come to God. It is not about having a perfect faith but a dependent faith. Jesus does not ask us to rid ourselves of all of our doubts before we can come to Him. He does not answer prayers only when they are prayed with perfect faith. Jesus calls us to come to Him with our imperfect faith and rest in His perfect grace. Instead of trying to muster up faith on our own, Jesus is the One who helps increase our faith. We cannot rid ourselves of doubt and unbelief in our own strength. We need to move toward Jesus, asking Him to help increase our faith and trust Him when we are struggling to believe. As we do, we can rest in His grace, knowing that He still loves us, even when we doubt.

The love and grace of Jesus also remind us that our salvation is secure, even in our doubts. Our salvation is not dependent on us having perfect faith, nor does the security of our salvation depend on us having perfect faith. It is Christ's grace that saves us, and it is by His grace, through the Spirit, that we are given faith to trust and believe in Him. It is His grace that continues to sustain us no matter how weak or strong our faith may be. Jesus will always welcome us to Him, even if we wrestle with questions and feelings of doubt. We can come to Him and trust that He will help us in every moment of unbelief.

We can come to Him and trust that He will help us in every moment of unbelief.

Day One — Questions

In what ways do you rely on your strength instead of relying on the strength of the Lord?
How does prayer help you relinquish your own self-sufficiency?

How does it comfort you to know that Jesus loves us, and helps us even when we doubt?
How does this truth encourage you to come to Him in moments of unbelief?

What are some doubts or truths about God and His Word that you are struggling with currently?
Spend some time in prayer, asking Jesus to help you in your unbelief.

True greatness is not about power or
position but about sacrifice and service.

True Greatness

Jesus has been teaching His disciples important discipleship lessons as they slowly make their journey to Jerusalem. This is no coincidence as Jesus is intentionally using the time He has left before His crucifixion to teach valuable truths about what it looks like to be a follower of Christ. As they journey in today's passage, Jesus uses the words and experiences of His disciples to teach how followers of Christ are to be humble and inclusive people. In doing so, they reflect the character of the God they follow, who is the very definition of humility and inclusivity.

Today's passage begins with Jesus informing His disciples about His death and resurrection for the second time. To speak and repeat these details to His disciples shows how Jesus wanted to continually remind His disciples of what was coming. Jesus is not hiding the events to come but revealing them to prepare the disciples' hearts, even if they do not understand His words quite yet.

As Jesus and His disciples journey, Jesus asks what the disciples have been discussing amongst themselves. They admit to Jesus that they have been debating who is the greatest among them. Jesus does not entertain their question by choosing a disciple who is the greatest. Instead, He redefines greatness. Jesus tells them that if anyone wants to be first, he must be last and a servant of all (Mark 9:35). In essence, Jesus teaches that true greatness is humility. Instead of pursuing greatness, followers of Christ are to surrender the desire to be great. Believers are to be servants who do not aspire to be the best or on "top" but who seek to serve and put others first. Jesus's teaching of greatness is the complete opposite of what our world defines as greatness. But that is the whole point! True greatness is not about power or position but about sacrifice and service.

The best example of this kind of humility is Jesus. Jesus is the ultimate servant of all. Jesus could have come to earth boasting of His greatness as God, but He did not. While He pointed to His greatness, He did not gloat about His greatness. Instead, He left His glorious position at the right hand of the Father to come to the earth as a servant, allowing Himself to be humbled to the point of death (Philippians 2:5–8). As believers, we reflect the humility and servitude of Christ when we humbly serve others and put them first.

Jesus uses an example of a child to demonstrate this teaching further. Children in that specific time period did not have prominent status in society. In comparison to the elite,

Week 4 Day 2 — 95

children were seen as being small and insignificant; therefore, they were an example of those who are "last." Yet Jesus encourages His disciples to welcome, serve, and care for children and all people who are considered to be the least. Jesus welcomed outcasts and misfits to Him. Therefore, so should we. As we do, we end up ultimately serving and glorifying the Lord.

Jesus then uses one of the disciples' experiences to continue His teaching of humility and inclusivity. The disciples tell Jesus how they tried to stop a man casting out demons in Jesus's name. They did so because this man was not part of the group of disciples. Jesus tells them to support this man and others like him—not stop him. The man's actions demonstrated how he was empowered by God, and therefore, he should not be stopped from doing works in Jesus's name. The man may be outside "the group," but that did not make him inferior or invaluable to God's kingdom. Jesus teaches how we are to treat believers who are different from us or do things differently than us with kindness and respect. We should never discount the faith and fruit of other believers, even if they are not affiliated with our Christian circles.

Jesus then warns about leading others away from their faith. Jesus gives the example of a child again to represent believers and says how it is wrong for a believer to cause other believers to stumble in their faith or to lead them away from Him. As believers, we are to come alongside brothers and sisters in Christ to spur them on in their faith, not create stumbling blocks in their faith. We can create these stumbling blocks by rejecting other believers, putting other believers down, or belittling their gifts. These stumbling blocks can have dire consequences. By shutting other believers down or shutting them out, we can cause their faith to weaken, or even worse, cause them to be led away from the faith.

Through these teachings, Jesus teaches us how disciples of Christ are people who walk in humility and pursue inclusivity. As disciples live this way, we show the love of Christ, spread the message of the gospel, and spur one another on in the faith. We can be people who lay greatness aside, just like Jesus did, who keep ourselves from desiring to make our names known, so Jesus's name can be known.

> As believers, we reflect the humility and servitude of Christ when we humbly serve others and put them first.

Day Two — Questions

In what ways do you see the world value greatness?

Do you find it easy or hard to put yourself last? How does this passage encourage your humility?

How have you seen believers be hurt and led away from their faith because of how other believers treated them? How can you be careful not to do the same?

The truth of the gospel that believers share and live out brings life into the corruption of this world.

A Vital Warning

Jesus concluded yesterday's passage with a warning not to cause other believers to stumble, and in today's passage, Jesus warns believers to keep themselves from stumbling. In doing so, Jesus teaches about the seriousness of sin that for some has eternal consequences.

Jesus uses a hyperbole, or an exaggerated statement, to teach about removing the stumbling blocks that keep someone from experiencing eternal life. Jesus says it is better to remove a hand, eye, or foot, and enter into the kingdom of God without them, than hold on to them and receive the consequence of hell. Jesus's reference to eyes, feet, and hands cover all the parts of someone that can lead them astray: what they see, where they go, and what they do.

This teaching of Jesus reveals the seriousness of sin. If someone clings to their sin instead of repenting from their sin, they will receive the punishment of hell. Therefore, the seriousness of sin is connected with the seriousness of hell. Jesus describes hell as a place "where their worm does not die, and the fire is not quenched" (Mark 9:48). His words teach how hell is a place of constant torment. If someone does not consider the consequences of their sin now, they will experience the consequence of hell for eternity.

This warning from Jesus should not scare those of us who are in Christ. The forgiveness we have received from Christ assures us that we have been rescued from the horror of hell. However, Jesus's words should cause believers to consider the sin in their lives that keep them from following Christ faithfully. While sinful eyes, feet, and hands are stumbling blocks to eternal life for unbelievers, sinful eyes, feet, and hands are stumbling blocks to discipleship for believers.

Believers have redeemed hearts but a sin nature, so we will still struggle to put sin to death daily. Jesus teaches in Mark 8:34 how following Him involves constantly denying oneself and picking up one's cross. For believers, the cutting off of hands, eyes, and feet in the passage involves putting to death the things in our lives that we value more than Christ. Every day, it is important for us to consider what we are doing with our eyes, hands, and feet. What are we looking at that we know we should not? Where do our feet take us that leads us into temptation? What do we do with our hands that causes us to sin? As believers, we should be serious about sin in our lives and vigilant to remove it, no matter how painful it may be, so we can pursue Jesus and walk in Christlikeness.

Jesus goes on to say in Mark 9:49 how everyone will be salted with fire. Here, Jesus teaches how those who do not follow Christ will experience the fires of punishment, but those who do follow Christ will experience the fires of purification. Fire and salt were two elements often used in sacrifices (Leviticus 2:13, 9:24). Jesus employs both of these elements as symbols to represent the sacrifice required to follow Christ. As we learned in Mark 8, following Jesus involves a cost, but the cost is always worthwhile.

By His grace, God uses the sacrifices we make to follow Christ, as well as the fires of trials and suffering, to shape us into the image of His Son. Believers are tested by trials of fire to be purified but to also give God glory. Just as a fiery sacrifice was an offering to the Lord, so are fiery trials opportunities for believers to glorify the Lord. As we make sacrifices for the Lord, we will be living sacrifices to the Lord (Romans 12:1).

Clinging to sinful desires taints our hearts, but obedience to the Lord purifies our hearts. As we continue to pursue Jesus and follow His commands, we will grow in our holiness and Christlikeness. We will find the things of this world that tempt our allegiance no longer have a hold on us. Following Christ and making sacrifices for Him not only does a work in our lives but also in the lives of others.

Jesus encourages believers in Mark 9:50 to have salt among each other and to be at peace with one another. Salt is a preservative that keeps food from rotting. In the same way, believers are to live in such a way that they keep the world around them from rotting away. Even though the world is sinful and broken, the truth of the gospel that believers share and live out brings life into the corruption of this world.

Jesus's teaching in this passage gives warning to both believers and nonbelievers. Those who do not know Christ can benefit greatly from evaluating what is keeping them from entering the kingdom of God. Losing the things of this world is better than gaining the horrors of hell. The invitation to follow Jesus and be rescued from this fate remains available right here and now.

This passage should also challenge believers to think critically about the sin in our lives that we cling to rather than surrender. Whatever it is that we are afraid of losing, it is worth the cost to gain Christ. Even though following Jesus involves sacrifice and suffering, who we are becoming and our eternal destination with Christ makes discipleship worthwhile. May the seriousness of sin and the seriousness of hell compel us to be faithful to Christ and share the hope of the gospel with those who are in desperate need of rescue.

Who we are becoming and our eternal destination with Christ makes discipleship worthwhile.

Day Three — Questions

Why is it hard for those who do not know Christ to give up sinful and worldly desires?

Are there any areas of sin (hands, eyes, feet) that are keeping you from following Christ more faithfully? Spend some time in prayer, confessing these sins to the Lord and asking for the Spirit's help to remove them from your life.

How does the seriousness of hell in this passage motivate your evangelism?

The more we seek Christ over fame, fortune, or our own desires, the more the treasures of this world will fade.

Inheriting Eternal Life

The disciples have learned what true greatness looks like. This call to humility is not a one-time teaching of Jesus but a teaching that He will continue to reiterate. In today's passage, we learn more about what humility looks like and how it is connected to eternal life with Christ.

Jesus first teaches about humility through a lesson about divorce. When Jesus is asked if it is lawful for a man to divorce his wife, Jesus responds by saying Moses permitted divorce due to the hardness of the Israelites' hearts. Jesus reminds the people that God's design for marriage is a permanent covenantal union. However, instead of humbly obeying God's command, the Israelites sought a way to get out of marriage. While Jesus affirms the permanent union of marriage in these verses, His grace and forgiveness cover those who have walked through divorce. It is also important to note that if you are in an abusive relationship, you absolutely should seek safety and the counsel of a trusted advisor (1 Corinthians 5:11–12). While the circumstances surrounding divorce are not always the same, Christ's grace and love remain the same. In humility, we can look to Him, no matter our earthly circumstances.

People then begin to bring their children to Jesus. The disciples rebuke these people, but Jesus welcomes the children to Him, takes them up in His arms, and blesses them. His response to the children is a visual display of what He taught the disciples in the previous chapter. Jesus taught His disciples to welcome people like children, and He displays that welcome as He invites the children into His arms.

Jesus goes on to teach how the way to enter the kingdom of God is to be like a child. To be like a child is to depend on and trust Jesus, just as a child depends on and trusts his parents. Children are hopeless and powerless without the guidance of their parents, and that is a picture of all of us without Jesus. If one desires to be a part of God's family and receive eternal life, they must be humble like a child by recognizing their need for Jesus.

This humble and meek position needed to receive salvation is further demonstrated as Jesus interacts with a rich, young ruler. This man approaches Jesus and asks what he must do to inherit eternal life. Jesus repeats the commands of God to the man, and the man replies that he has kept them all. But Jesus sees the area of the man's life that is hindering his ability to enter into God's kingdom. Jesus tells the man he needs to let go of his possessions and sell all he has to the poor.

The man's grief in response to Jesus's words reveals how tightly he holds on to his possessions and how his identity is wrapped up in what he has. This man came to the right source, Jesus, to inquire about how to be saved, but the love of his possessions kept him from receiving salvation. This man's response reminds us of the example of the seed choked by thorns in Jesus's teaching from Mark 4:7. The things of this world prevented this man from obtaining the eternal life that Jesus offered him.

The man's question and response also point to how people often try to earn salvation. This man said, "What must I do to inherit eternal life?" (verse 17). This man had tried to "do" by keeping God's commands, perhaps thinking the riches he accumulated earned him a position in God's kingdom. Yet neither money nor morality was enough to satisfy his need for salvation. This man is like so many people today who believe that what they do or what they have grants them entrance into God's family. Money nor morality can satisfy or save—only the blood of Jesus can.

Jesus takes this opportunity to teach His disciples a lesson about God's kingdom and the power of God's grace. He uses an analogy of a camel and a needle to describe how difficult it is for a rich person to enter into the kingdom of God. Why? It is difficult for the wealthy to enter the kingdom of God because, unlike children, it is easy for pride to keep them from recognizing their need for Christ. They do not come with open hands like a child does—eager to grasp onto Jesus with trust and dependency. Instead, they often hold tight to the riches they have acquired, afraid to let go of what they have. This is not to say that those who have been blessed with wealth cannot enter God's kingdom, but rather, the analogy serves as a warning to believers not to fall into the trap of chasing after riches to find fulfillment.

However, when the disciples ask, "Then who can be saved?" Jesus answers by reminding them that with God, all things are possible. Jesus teaches that we cannot save ourselves, for it is God's grace given through Jesus Christ that provides salvation. Anyone who places their faith in Jesus and repents from their sin will be saved by the power of the Spirit within them.

Like the rich man, we too can place our identity in the things of this world. Even if we have entered into a relationship with Christ, our pursuit of Christ can be hindered as we seek our identity apart from Him. Today's passage connects back to Jesus's teaching that we must deny ourselves and take up our cross to follow Him (Mark 8:34). Part of that process is daily placing our identity in Jesus and recognizing where we are searching for our source of security and satisfaction.

The more we seek Christ over fame, fortune, or our own desires, the more the treasures of this world will fade. Jesus says in verses 29–31 how those who pay the cost to follow Him will receive greater eternal gain. While persecution will be a part of following Jesus, the eternal gain is worth the temporary pain. When we let go of the treasures of this world, our hands are freed to grasp onto Jesus and the rich life we have in Him.

When we let go of the treasures of this world, our hands are freed to grasp onto Jesus.

Day Four — Questions

Read 2 Corinthians 8:8—9 and Ephesians 2:4—7. In what ways does Christ make us "rich"?

Read Matthew 6:19—24. What are some things your heart treasures? How can you store up treasures in heaven instead of storing up treasures on earth?

Read Philippians 3:7—11. How is gaining Christ worth the loss of the things of this world? What are some things you need to lose or let go of so your identity and pursuit are in Christ alone?

Jesus did not come to be served but to serve by giving up His life to save sinners from the punishment of their sins.

Glory & Humility

Throughout the past several chapters, Mark has been piecing together accounts that speak to the themes of humility and servitude. In today's passage, we see those themes present again through an interaction Jesus has with His disciples as well as an encounter with a blind man. However, it is the inclusion of Jesus's triumphal entry in Jerusalem that brings all of these ideas together as Jesus demonstrates both glory and humility as He makes His way to the cross.

Jesus has already made two predictions of His death and resurrection to His disciples, and today, Jesus makes His third and final prediction. Each one of these predictions has been followed by an interaction with the disciples that demonstrates their unbelief and lack of humility. The third prediction follows that same pattern as the disciples, specifically James and John, make a high demand from Jesus.

After Jesus predicts His death and resurrection, James and John request to sit at either side of Jesus in heaven. Their desire for a position of glory reveals how they have not taken Jesus's teachings about humility to heart. Jesus asks James and John if they are willing to drink the cup He will drink and be baptized with the same baptism He will experience. The cup and baptism represent the suffering and death Jesus will experience on the cross. In essence, Jesus is asking: *Are you willing to experience deep suffering and death to receive glory?* The disciples do not understand the seriousness of Jesus's question, so they answer that they are willing. Jesus responds by confirming that James and John will go on to experience suffering and death for His name, but God decides who will sit in a high position with Christ.

Jesus then reiterates what true glory looks like. He reminds the disciples that they are not to be people who desire a position of power and glory but people who desire a position of humble service. Why? Because Jesus did not come to be served but to serve by giving up His life to save sinners from the punishment of their sins (Mark 10:45). He did not come to gain power but to give power away.

The pathway to glory involves suffering. Philippians 2:5–11 teaches us how Jesus left His high position of glory to be a humble servant, but God raised Jesus from the dead and exalted Him to His right hand. Jesus chose to experience the pathway of suffering before returning to His position of glory. In doing so, He demonstrates what true servanthood looks like. As believers, what matters is not a position of glory in this life but our eternal glory in the life to come. Second Corinthians 4:17 says, "For our momentary light affliction is producing for us an absolutely incomparable eternal weight of glory." Following Jesus involves sacrifice and suffering, but our suffering is not in vain. One day, we will experience eternal glory with Christ, a reality and position not by our doing but by what Christ has done for us.

The experience with the disciples contrasts Jesus's encounter with a blind beggar. The blind beggar calls Jesus the Son of David, publicly proclaiming how Jesus is the fulfillment of the Messianic King promised from David's line (2 Samuel 7:12). When Jesus approaches the blind man, He asks the same question He asked His disciples — "What do you want me to do for you?" (Mark 10:51) — to which the man replies that he wants to receive his sight. This blind man contrasts the disciples' request because his request was humble rather than selfish. This man also represents the lowly position Jesus just described. He had a low position as a blind beggar, but he chose to come to Jesus and not ask for glory but mercy.

Jesus then goes to make His triumphal entry in Jerusalem. This passage fulfills Zechariah 9:9, which says, "Rejoice greatly, Daughter Zion! Shout in triumph, Daughter Jerusalem! Look, your King is coming to you; he is righteous and victorious, humble and riding on a donkey, on a colt, the foal of a donkey." Jesus's entry through Jerusalem is a display of His kingship but also His humility as He comes in riding not on a noble steed but a lowly donkey.

This entry marks a pivotal point in Jesus's ministry as it demonstrates Jesus's pathway of suffering to glory. The people in this passage cry out to Jesus, "Hosanna!" which means "save us" (Mark 11:9–10) The people of Israel were waiting for the promised Messianic King who would bring restoration to God's people and establish His kingdom on earth. By this triumphal entry, Jesus declares that He is the fulfillment of the Messianic King, yet He will save sinners in a way that they did not expect. The people desired for the Messiah to save them from the oppressive government, but Jesus will save them from their bondage to sin — not in a display of glory but in a display of humility as He will lay naked on the cross.

The triumphal entry reveals how Jesus is our humble King, and the response of the blind beggar teaches us how we should approach our humble King. We should not come to Jesus to get anything from Him but mercy. We do not come to Jesus so He can make us wealthy, popular, or happy — we come to Jesus so He can make us whole. The disciples thought they were entitled to a position of glory, but what they needed was Christ's grace. Because of our sin, we are not entitled to anything other than death. It is only through Christ that we can have salvation. Therefore, let us see Jesus not as a genie who grants us wishes but as a King who grants us mercy. May we serve Him with humility and gratitude, sharing His mercy with others as we live as servants of all.

We come to Jesus so He
can make us whole.

Day Five — Questions

In what ways do you struggle with being served rather than being the one to serve?
How does this passage encourage you to lay down these desires?

Read Philippians 2:1—11. How are you to live in light of Christ's humiliation and exaltation?

Compare and contrast the request of the disciples and the request of the blind beggar.
How do these requests impact what our prayer requests to God should and should not be like?

"Whoever wants to become great among you will be your servant, and whoever wants to be first among you will be a slave to all. For even the Son of Man did not come to be served, but to serve, and to give his life as a ransom for many."

MARK 10:43B–45

Week Four — Reflection

Summarize the main points from this week's Scripture readings.

What did you observe from this week's passages about God and His character?

What do this week's passages reveal about the condition of mankind and yourself?

How do these passages point to the gospel?

How should you respond to these passages? What specific action steps can you take this week to apply them in your life?

Write a prayer in response to your study of God's Word. Adore God for who He is, confess sins He revealed in your own life, ask Him to empower you to walk in obedience, and pray for anyone who comes to mind as you study.

True worship would not be possible
without the work of Jesus on the cross.

Lessons from a Fig Tree

Jesus has made His triumphal entry into Jerusalem, declaring that He is the fulfillment of the promised Messianic King. Yesterday's text ended with Jesus looking around the temple, and in today's text, we see Jesus interact with the temple in a much greater way. Sandwiched between this event at the temple are two lessons from a fig tree that may seem disconnected from the temple experience on the surface. However, it is through these lessons from the fig tree that we see the meaning of Jesus's temple experience more clearly, as we learn the power of prayer, the gift of access to God, and what true worship looks like.

Jesus and His disciples are on the way to Jerusalem, and Jesus is hungry. Jesus sees a fig tree with leaves from the distance and goes to see if it has fruit. When Jesus gets to the fig tree, He sees how the tree has leaves but no fruit. In response, Jesus curses the fig tree, saying that it will never bear fruit again. Mark records that the disciples heard Jesus's words, and we can only imagine the confusion they must have had. Why would Jesus curse a tree?

Without the next experience in the temple, we would not understand the depths of Jesus's words. Jesus and His disciples leave this place and go to the temple. Mark records an almost instantaneous reaction from Jesus as He throws out the money changers in the temple and overturns their tables. Why is Jesus doing this? The area that Jesus and His disciples entered was likely the outer court of the temple, the Court of the Gentiles. Gentiles were not allowed to enter the inner court of the temple, so it was here in the outer court where Gentiles would come for prayer. Yet the markets that people set up in the court prevented the Gentiles from having a space for reverent prayer. Instead of having a quiet place for prayer, the space was full of people and the noise of sellers seeking to make money.

Jesus's reaction is a righteous response to the actions of the people. God's house, the temple, was designed to be a place of reverent worship and prayer. God's temple, along with the worship from His people, was also designed to be a light to the nations. The glory of the temple and the worship of God's people invited those who did not know God to come and know Him. However, the display of markets and the greed of the merchants prevented the worship of non-Jews. These people were making themselves an obstacle to worship for the Gentiles, proving they had no reverence for God, only selfish and greedy desires.

It is through this encounter at the temple that we understand Jesus's experience with the fig tree. The fig tree represents the nation of Israel and their withered worship. A fig tree with leaves and no fruit was a sign of decay; therefore, the fig tree represents the spiritual decay of Israel and Israel's hollow religiosity. The people of Israel were God's chosen people, yet their hearts were far from Him. They boasted of their status as God's people, but they failed to bear fruit as His people because of their sin and unbelief.

The nation of Israel rejected and desecrated their access to God, but Jesus goes on to teach how believers can embrace their access to God. Jesus uses the figurative language of a mountain being thrown into the sea to teach about the power of prayer. As believers, we value our access to God when we come to God in prayer. However, our worship withers when we turn away from God instead of praying to Him. Jesus's promise that our prayers will be answered is connected to the kind of prayers we pray. The more we grow in our faith and obey the Lord, the more our desires will align with God's desires. Our prayers will be shaped by the desire for God's will to be done, not our own will, and God grants every prayer that aligns with His will.

Today's passage encourages true worship. Yet, true worship would not be possible without the work of Jesus on the cross. Jesus's sacrifice on the cross covered the punishment of our sin and satisfied God's wrath. With God's wrath satisfied, our sin no longer separates us from Him. Jesus clearing out the obstacles of worship in the temple is a picture of what Jesus does for every heart that is transformed by the gospel. Christ's grace removes the barrier between us and God, giving us complete and permanent access to the Lord. Now anyone, Jew or Gentile, can come to know and worship God.

The lessons from the fig tree encourage us to think critically about our own worship. Are we rejoicing in our access to God by worshiping Him? Or are we worshiping God with our lips but not our lives? If we find ourselves struggling to worship the Lord, or if we find areas where our worship to God has become hypocritical, we must remember the gospel. We must remember the lengths Jesus took so that we could have access to God. We keep our worship of God from withering as we bask in the light of the gospel.

As believers, we should also remember that with the Holy Spirit inside of us, we are the new temple. Our access to God means that we can worship Him wherever we go, and our worship to God is an invitation for others to know and worship Him. Our sinful nature will cause us to struggle with dedicated worship to God, but we have the Holy Spirit within us to help us. As we daily rely on and rest in the power of the Spirit, we will worship God rightly, and we will be a light for the nations, inviting others to know the God who loves them.

Christ's grace removes the barrier between us and God, giving us complete and permanent access to the Lord.

How does hypocritical worship act as a barrier for others coming to know Jesus?
How can you keep worship to God genuine in your life?

How does having full access to God impact your prayer life? How does your relationship with God and the character of God encourage boldness in prayer?

What is keeping you from worshiping God as you should? Are there any idols (greed, materialism, pride, status, etc.) that are obstacles in your worship? Spend some time in prayer, asking God to remove any obstacles to your worship, and ask for the Spirit's help to walk in faithfulness and true worship to God.

Jesus, the beloved Son, was sent by the authority of God to accomplish salvation.

A Confrontation About Authority

READ MARK 11:27–12:17

Our world holds different views on authority. Some people willingly submit to authority, while others tend to rebel against authority. Often, a person's character is reflected by how they view and treat authority. In today's passage, we look at three out of multiple confrontations the Sanhedrin had with Jesus, and as we do, we learn more about these religious leaders' character, as well as the ultimate authority of God.

As Jesus and His disciples are walking in the temple, the chief priests, scribes, and the elders approach Jesus. These three groups of people comprised the Sanhedrin, a religious council of seventy-one members who handled religious matters between the Roman government and the Jews. This is the first time that Jesus has been approached by the Sanhedrin, and the location of this approach is no coincidence. Jesus is in the temple, the most authoritative place in Israel, being confronted by the most authoritative body in Israel. Yet it is through these confrontations that Jesus will demonstrate His ultimate authority.

The Sanhedrin asks Jesus by what and whose authority Jesus does these things. We can surmise by the previous passage that the religious leaders are most likely talking about Jesus's actions in the temple. Jesus's actions of clearing away the market tables was an act of authority, displaying to those around Him God's power to remove sin and wickedness. But the Sanhedrin question Jesus's actions. Instead of giving them a direct answer, Jesus responds with a question, which was a common argumentation method amongst rabbinical teachers. Jesus asks the Sanhedrin if John's baptism was from heaven or of human origin.

Jesus's question may seem disconnected from the Sanhedrin's question, but it actually answers the Sanhedrin's question. Christ's baptism by John was a prominent demonstration of Christ's authority. Through Christ's baptism, Jesus was empowered for His ministry, and the voice of God affirmed Christ's identity as God. Jesus's question gave the Sanhedrin an option. Would they say that John's baptism was from man alone, with no evidence of God's power? Or would they say that John's baptism was from heaven, an act of God's power? If the Sanhedrin said by human power, they would discount the beliefs of many Jews who affirmed the authority of John, but if they said by heaven, then they would affirm Christ's authority from God. Fearing the crowd around them, the Sanhedrin dodge a direct answer by saying they do not know. Because the Sanhedrin responds in this way, Jesus tells them that He will not answer their question.

Jesus then goes on to tell a parable that continues a lesson on authority. In this parable, the owner is God, the vineyard is Israel, the tenants are the religious leaders, the servants are the prophets, and the beloved son is Jesus. Through this parable, Jesus confronts the hypocritical leadership of the Sanhedrin. He teaches how God had entrusted servants to guide and lead Israel, but Israel's leaders rejected these servants, causing the nation of Israel to be led astray. God's long-suffering is demonstrated by the owner's choice to keep sending servants. With the servants killed, the owner sends his beloved son, but the tenants conspire to kill him too, thinking they will receive the inheritance of the vineyard if they do. This scenario represents how God has sent His beloved Son, Jesus, to save Israel, yet their leaders, as well as many of the people, reject Him and will ultimately kill Him.

Jesus quotes from Psalm 118:22–23 to teach how the religious leaders of Israel reject Jesus but cannot ruin God's plan. Even though Jesus is rejected and will eventually be killed, God will accomplish His plan of salvation and redemption through Jesus. The rejection of Jesus will cause those who do not repent and believe in Him to be punished, but those who repent and believe will rejoice over God's work of salvation through Christ, proclaiming this "is wonderful in our eyes" (Mark 12:11, Psalm 118:23).

In the last confrontation, the Sanhedrin tries to trap Jesus by asking Him if it is lawful to pay taxes. Jesus tells them to give to Caesar what is Caesar's and give to God the things that are God's. Jesus's answer reveals how the Messiah will not overthrow the government in the way the Jewish people expect. Jesus reveals His respect for the government while also affirming God's authority over the government.

These three interactions reveal the authority of Jesus. First, Jesus has the authority to say and do things that make Him equal with God because He is God, and His baptism confirms this truth. Second, Jesus, the beloved Son, was sent by the authority of God to accomplish salvation, and His authority would still be maintained and proclaimed, even with the people's rejection. Lastly, Jesus confirms God's authority over the government, and therefore, His own authority over the government. Through these interactions, we learn that humble submission leads to life, but prideful rejection leads to death. The religious leaders' pride and unbelief were a stumbling block that prevented them from receiving Christ's salvation. But those who submit to Jesus receive Christ's salvation.

As believers, we live in continual submission to Christ's authority. We submit to Christ's authority when we confess Him as our Lord and Savior, but daily, we live out this confession of submission by serving Jesus and obeying Him. We live out Christ's teaching of dying to ourselves as we lay down our inclination to be the ones who control our lives. Daily, we are to choose to submit to God and what His Word commands of us. This can be hard as we live in a world that wants to make its own rules of living. But as we submit to our ultimate authority, God and His Word, we will be people of humble submission, declaring to the world how following Jesus is better than pursuing our own agenda.

Day Two — Questions

Read 1 Peter 2:7–10. How are we to live as believers in light of this passage?

In what ways do you struggle to obey God's authority? Why is submitting to God better than following your own plans and desires?

How does Jesus's response in Mark 12:17 reveal how believers should respond to the authority of the government? Why is it important that we respond in this way? Consider Romans 13:1 as you answer the questions.

Jesus can act and speak with authority
because He is God in the flesh.

Jesus has been placed in the figurative boxing ring with the Sanhedrin, and with every test and confrontation, Jesus has fought back with words of wisdom and truth. In today's passage, we see this questioning battle finish. As Jesus answers these final questions and asks a question of His own, Jesus reveals His identity as Messiah, as well as the importance of loving God and His Word.

The Sadducees are the next group of people to approach Jesus. The Sadducees did not believe in the resurrection of the dead, and one of the main reasons was because they only read and affirmed the Torah, the first five books of the Old Testament. They believed that the Torah did not say anything about resurrection, so it must not be true. The Sadducees decide to question Jesus about resurrection. They use a far-fetched argument about a woman who continues to marry after each spouse dies. The Pharisees believed that marriage would still exist after death, so the Sadducees use this argument against resurrection. If life after death was real and marriage after death remained, the woman in this situation would have a lot of husbands after death.

Jesus reveals how the Sadducees' argument is illogical. Jesus says the Sadducees are flawed in their understanding and beliefs because they do not know the Scriptures or the power of God. If they truly knew the Scriptures, they would affirm all of God's Word as the Word of God, and they would see how the Scriptures affirm resurrection. Jesus tells the Sadducees there will be no marriage in heaven, so the situation they have presented in their argument will not exist. He also quotes from Exodus 3:6 as an example of Scripture's affirmation of resurrection. In Exodus 3:6, God tells Moses that He is the God of Abraham, Issac, and Jacob. The present tense verb, as well as Jesus's statement that "He is not the God of the dead but of the living" (verse 27), reveals how God's people—like Abraham, Issac, and Jacob—are not dead but have been raised to eternal life with God.

After this questioning, a scribe comes to Jesus and asks Him which command is the most important out of all of the commands in Scripture. Jesus responds by quoting Deuteronomy 6:4–5 and Leviticus 19:18, which say to love the Lord and love your neighbor as yourself. The scribe affirms what Jesus has said and even adds that obeying these commands is more important than burnt sacrifices. Jesus tells the man that he is not far from the kingdom of God because of his words. Unlike other scribes or the Sanhedrin, this man recognized what matters most: loving God and loving others.

Mark reveals in verse 34 that after this questioning, no one dared to question Him anymore. Now, it is time for Jesus to ask a question. Jesus asks why the scribes say that the Messiah is the son of David. Jesus quotes Psalm 110:1, which describes David, through the power of the Holy Spirit, understanding that the Messiah was God. The scribes believed that the Messiah would be human because he was the "son" of David. But by this verse, Jesus proclaims how the Messiah is both human and divine. Jesus is the Son of David and the Son of God. This short lesson from Jesus is a public display of His identity, and His words connect with yesterday's passage on authority. Jesus can act and speak with authority because He is God in the flesh.

Jesus then goes on to warn about the scribes. He says to beware of scribes who care only about their status, attention, and position. Jesus shows how the scribes care about attention and position by describing their long robes, their expectation to receive greetings in public, their desire for the best seats and places of honor, and their habit of praying long prayers for show. Jesus reveals how the scribes care more about their position than caring for the lowly. They devour widow's homes instead of taking care of widows. These words from Jesus affirm the failure of the religious leaders to follow the first and second commandments. They loved themselves more than they loved God, and they failed to show love to their neighbor.

Contrasted with the haughty scribes is a humble widow. Jesus and His disciples observe the rich placing large sums of money in a temple treasury, but a poor widow puts in two coins. Jesus tells His disciples that this woman, although she physically gave less, gave more in the eyes of the Lord because she gave all that she had. This widow shows a genuine love for the Lord by her sacrificial giving.

Jesus's interactions with the people in this passage reveal to us what is important: loving God and loving others. It can be hard to love God with all of who we are because our flesh seeks to worship ourselves and pursue worldly desires. But when we consider the love that Jesus has shown us on the cross, the desire for self-worship dissipates. We love God with all we are in response to the great love He has shown us. In the moments we struggle to obey God's commands, we must focus on loving God with all of who we are. It is out of a love for God first that obedience to Him flows. Unlike the Sadducees who failed to know God's Word, our love for God is cultivated as we know and study His Word. Remaining close to God and His Word keeps our hearts from chasing after other pursuits. And the more we love God and rest in His love, the more we will love those around us. A heart that loves God cannot help but show love to others.

A heart that loves God cannot help but show love to others.

How does Jesus's statement, "He is not the God of the dead but of the living" (verse 27), connect with the three predictions He has given His disciples? What does this mean for believers?

In the table below, write what you think it means to love the Lord with your heart, soul, mind, and strength in the first column. Then, write how you can live that out practically this week in the second column.

HEART		
SOUL		
MIND		
STRENGTH		

How does the widow's sacrifice encourage you to make sacrifices for the Lord?
What are some practical ways you can sacrifice for the Lord?

The Spirit empowers us and
will carry us through to
our eternity with Christ.

Signs of the End

READ MARK 13

End-times theology and teaching can be confusing, and for many, thinking about the end times can be scary. Mark 13 can be a hard passage to understand because, like many other prophecies in Scripture, it is not always clear exactly how and when these events will take place. Even though there are differences in opinion on the exact details of Jesus's teaching, what we learn from Mark 13 is the hope of Christ's coming in the midst of hardship, as well as the importance of remaining alert and firm as we await Christ's return.

Mark 13 opens with the disciples commenting to Jesus about the grandeur of the temple. Jesus responds by predicting how all these stones that the disciples have admired will be demolished. Jesus's prediction of the temple destruction ended up coming true in AD 70. What becomes difficult, then, is knowing if the rest of what Jesus speaks about in this chapter is connected to the temple destruction in AD 70 or connected to end-time events. Many people disagree with how to interpret these teachings, but one strong possibility is that Jesus was adopting a similar method of prophecy like the prophets in the Old Testament, who gave predictions with both a partial near fulfillment and a future full fulfillment.

The disciples ask Jesus when these things will happen and what signs to look out for. Instead of giving the disciples a time, Jesus calls His disciples to watch out for deceivers. He tells the disciples not to be deceived by those who claim to be the Messiah but are not. In verse 9, Jesus calls His disciples to be vigilant once again as He tells them that they will face persecution for their faith.

Amongst this warning is encouragement that the Holy Spirit will be with those who face persecution. Jesus also promises in verse 13 that those who endure to the end will be saved. As believers, we will face persecution in various forms because of our faith in Christ. Even though persecution is difficult, the possibility of persecution should not deter us from sharing the gospel and living out our faith. It is necessary for the gospel to be preached to all nations, even if we are rejected or persecuted for doing so. We can be cheered, even in persecution, knowing that the Spirit empowers us and will carry us through to our eternity with Christ.

Perhaps one of the most difficult parts of Mark 13 to understand is verses 14–21. The "abomination of desolation" that Jesus speaks of in verse 14 can be hard to interpret.

Some commentators believe that the abomination of desolation refers to the destruction of the temple, whereas others believe it refers to the anti-Christ who will bring about destruction at the end of the age. What we can surmise from the text is that whether or not this is a near fulfillment or a future fulfillment, the events involve God's people experiencing tribulation. Yet again, we see a glimmer of hope and encouragement as Jesus says these days will be short for the sake of God's chosen people.

Among these prophecies of destruction and tribulation is a prophecy of Christ's future coming. Jesus says that after the tribulation, He will come in a display of power and glory to collect those who are saved. The disciples, as well as believers today, can be encouraged by Jesus's words. At times, it can feel as if we will live in this broken world forever, but Jesus will not leave us in this place of suffering. One day, He will return and bring all believers to Himself, ushering us into the new heaven and new earth to live in a world without sin or pain forever.

Jesus also reminds us of God's eternality in this passing world. Thinking about the tribulation in this chapter can leave us scared, but there is hope to cling to amidst this foretelling of suffering. The things of this world may pass away, but God and His Word remain. And because, as believers, we belong to our eternal God, we can stand firm in the midst of hardship, knowing that our eternity with God is secure.

Lastly, Jesus reminds us that only God knows the timing of these events. Many people today and in the past have tried to predict the end of the age, but they have always been wrong. Instead of getting caught up in these predictions, we should remain focused on doing God's work. Jesus gives His last admonition in verses 33–37, saying three times that we should be alert. We should not allow the uncertainty of the timing of Christ's return to cause us to be lax. Instead, we are to act as if Christ can return at any minute, and we are to use the time He has given us to live and work for Him.

While the timing and exact execution of these events remain uncertain, what we do know is that Jesus commands and calls us to be people who are alert and on guard. We will encounter people and teachings that assume beliefs about the end times that find no grounding in Scripture, but we keep ourselves from being swayed by these teachings as we cling to the eternal Word of God. As we remain rooted in God's Word and use the time in the present to work for the Lord, we look ahead at what is to come, not in fear but in hope. Jesus is coming back for us, and we will spend eternity with Him.

The things of this world may pass away, but God and His Word remain.

Day Four — Questions

What is your usual response to end-times teaching? How does this chapter give you hope and comfort in light of the end times?

How does this chapter encourage you to persevere in evangelism and during times of suffering?

What does it look like practically for you to be alert and on guard?

By Jesus's sacrifice, those who repent
and believe in Him are forgiven of their sins
and given a right relationship with God.

The Passover Lamb

READ MARK 14:1–26

The time for Jesus's death is nearing, and we see evidence of this as the scribes and Pharisees plot to arrest and kill Jesus. They withhold their arrest for now, but with the help of Judas, it is only a matter of time before the religious leaders make their move. While the Pharisees and scribes are plotting, Jesus receives a special anointing and shares a significant meal with His disciples.

Jesus and His disciples are at Simon the leper's house when a woman comes to Jesus with a jar of perfume and pours it over Jesus's head. The disciples scold the woman for wasting perfume that she could have sold to feed the poor. Unlike those around Him, Jesus commends the woman for her act. Jesus says that she has done a noble thing by expressing her devotion to Him by this action. However, Jesus reveals a deeper significance to this woman's actions. While this most likely was not the woman's intention, Jesus says that this woman has anointed Jesus's body in advance for His burial. Not only this but as the gospel has spread, many will be told of this woman's actions.

The rest of today's passage is all about the Passover. The Passover was a significant festival for the Jewish people. This festival celebrated God's great work of releasing the Israelites from slavery in Egypt (Exodus 13:17–14:31). God's plan for delivering the Israelites involved various plagues, and the last plague was death. In the exodus from slavery, God commanded the Israelites to slaughter a lamb and paint the blood around their doorposts. As God went through Egypt, He would kill the firstborn of any house that did not have the blood. But for those who did have blood on their doorposts, God passed over the house and spared the child.

The process of Jesus's betrayal, death, and resurrection happening over the course of a Passover weekend is significant. Before God redeemed His people from slavery, a lamb was sacrificed. In the same way, God's plan of redemption involved the sacrifice of the ultimate Passover Lamb, Jesus Christ. Jesus took our place by sacrificing Himself on the cross. His blood was poured out for us, and because of His blood, we are saved from death.

By celebrating the Passover with His disciples, Jesus reveals the significance of His coming death. Jesus breaks the bread that was part of the Passover meal and says that this bread is His body. Jesus is not claiming the bread is literally His body, but the bread represents what will happen to Jesus's body on the cross. Just as the bread was broken, so will Jesus's body be broken on the cross.

Jesus also takes the cup and says that this is the blood of the covenant. Again, the wine in the cup is not Jesus's literal blood, but it represents the blood that Jesus will pour out on the cross. The covenant Jesus describes most likely refers to the new covenant that God promised in Jeremiah 31. The new covenant promised a relationship of faithfulness and intimacy between God and man, made possible by the forgiveness of their sins. Jesus's death on the cross inaugurated this covenant. By Jesus's sacrifice, those who repent and believe in Him are forgiven of their sins and given a right relationship with God.

This supper with the disciples points to Jesus's death to come, but it also points to Christ's future return. In verse 25, Jesus speaks of another supper to come, referred to as the Marriage Feast of the Lamb in Revelation 19:6–9. The Marriage Feast of the Lamb will be the celebration of God's people uniting with their Savior in the new heaven and new earth. When Christ returns, all believers will feast with their God in a world cleansed from sin.

The meal the disciples partook with Christ is a meal we continue to share today as believers. The Lord's Supper is a time when we gather together as believers to remember and reflect on what Christ has done for us. First Corinthians 11:26 tells us, "For as often as you eat this bread and drink the cup, you proclaim the Lord's death until he comes." We proclaim our Savior's death and resurrection as we share this meal together, remembering His body that was broken for us and His blood that was poured out for us. While the Lord's Supper is a significant time of remembrance, every day is an opportunity to remember and reflect on Christ's sacrifice.

Remembering Christ's sacrifice reminds us of what we could not do. We could not save ourselves from the punishment of death, but Jesus stepped in and took our place. He died so that we would never receive the punishment of eternal death. Christ's sacrifice also reminds us of the finality of our salvation. Jesus's sacrifice fully satisfied God's wrath, meaning the forgiveness we have is permanent. We may wrestle with feeling truly forgiven at times, but Christ's sacrifice affirms that we are forever forgiven. Remembering Christ's sacrifice also reminds us that we have been brought into the new covenant. We have been reconciled to God and given a relationship of joy and intimacy with Him that will never be taken away. All of these blessings are a gift of grace bought for us by Christ's body and blood. Praise be to our Passover Lamb!

Christ's sacrifice affirms that we are forever forgiven.

What does it say about God's character that He would provide redemption through Christ?

Read Exodus 12:1—6 and 1 Peter 1:19. How is Jesus our Passover Lamb?

Why is it important to remember Christ's death on the cross? How can you daily remember and reflect on Christ's sacrifice?

"Love the Lord your God with all your heart, with all your soul, with all your mind, and with all your strength. The second is, Love your neighbor as yourself. There is no other command greater than these."

MARK 12:30–31

Week Five — Reflection

Summarize the main points from this week's Scripture readings.

What did you observe from this week's passages about God and His character?

What do this week's passages reveal about the condition of mankind and yourself?

How do these passages point to the gospel?

How should you respond to these passages? What specific action steps can you take this week to apply them in your life?

Write a prayer in response to your study of God's Word. Adore God for who He is, confess sins He revealed in your own life, ask Him to empower you to walk in obedience, and pray for anyone who comes to mind as you study.

Sacrifice reveals love, and Jesus's sacrifice
on the cross is the greatest display
of love we could ever receive.

If you knew you were going to die, how would you use the time you had left? The clock is ticking for Jesus's impending arrest and death, but Jesus uses the hours He has remaining intentionally. In the previous passage, we saw Jesus share a meal with His disciples and speak to the sacrifice He would make on the cross. In today's passage, Jesus prepares His disciples' hearts by a sad prediction and uses the minutes leading up to His betrayal in prayer.

The previous passage ended joyfully as the disciples concluded their Passover meal with a hymn. Sadly, this passage begins more sorrowfully as Jesus predicts His disciples' future actions. Jesus tells His disciples that when He is arrested and killed, all of them will fall away from Him. Jesus quotes a passage from Zechariah 13:7 to describe how the disciples will scatter like sheep as their Shepherd is betrayed and killed. Jesus's arrest and death will test the disciples' faith, and by Jesus's prediction, the disciples' faith will not be strong enough. Rather than remaining strong with Jesus until the end, their unbelief and fear will cause them to run.

Yet amidst this sad prediction is a note of hope. Verse 28 reveals that even though the disciples will scatter at Jesus's death, they will be united again after Jesus's resurrection. Peter swears that he will not fall away even if the others fall away, but Jesus tells Peter that he will deny Jesus three times that very night. Despite these predictions, Peter, as well as the other disciples, insist that they will not deny Jesus.

Contrasted with the falling away of Jesus's disciples in the face of death is Christ's unwavering obedience in the face of death. The disciples have come to a place called Gethsemane, and it is here that we learn Jesus's three responses as He prepares to die.

First, Jesus experiences grief. Mark reveals how Jesus was deeply distressed and troubled, and Jesus tells Peter, James, and John that He is deeply grieved to the point of death (Mark 14:33–34). Jesus's reaction to His coming death is not a sign that Jesus was unaware of what He was going to do. He knew the Father's plan and had revealed the Father's plan several times to His disciples. Jesus's deep grief and distress was a demonstration of the agony that Jesus knew He would face on the cross, particularly the weight of our sin upon Him and the separation He would experience from His Father. Jesus's grief reveals just how real and costly His death on the cross will be.

Second, Jesus responds with prayer. Jesus falls on His knees to pray, a sign of deep spiritual anguish. But it is His deep spiritual anguish that moves Christ to prayer. What does He pray for? Jesus prays for God to take the cup from Him. Throughout Scripture, the cup was a metaphor of God's wrath that He would pour out upon the wicked and unrepentant (Ezekiel 23:32–34). Jesus would experience this cup of wrath poured out upon Him on the cross as He would take on the punishment of our sin in our place. In essence, Jesus is praying that God would make another way for Him to accomplish God's salvation plan.

However, through this prayer, we see Jesus's third response — obedience. Paired with Jesus's honest plea to God is a prayer of complete obedience to God's will. Jesus says to God, "Nevertheless, not what I will, but what you will" (Mark 14:36). Jesus's prayer to God reveals Jesus's obedience to the Father and His willingness to fulfill the Father's will and plan — no matter the cost.

Jesus spends much time in prayer before His arrest, but what are His disciples doing? They are sleeping. Jesus encourages His disciples to remain vigilant in prayer three times, but they let themselves fall asleep instead. Jesus speaks to Peter directly, saying to him, "Stay awake and pray so that you won't enter into temptation. The spirit is willing, but the flesh is weak" (Mark 14:38). Jesus's words to Peter connect with the prediction Jesus had made for Peter. Jesus had just told Peter how he will deny Him, but instead of praying that God will give him the strength to resist the desire to flee, Peter is sleeping. His spirit may have been willing to stick with Jesus, but without God's power that Peter could access through prayer, Peter was left with his flesh weak and vulnerable. As Jesus finishes His prayer, He tells His disciples to wake up, for the time of His betrayal and arrest has finally come.

As we consider Jesus's time in the garden of Gethsemane, we should be deeply encouraged by Christ's love for us. While obedience to God moved Jesus to the cross, Christ's love for us also moved Him to the cross. First John 3:16 tells us, "This is how we have come to know love: He laid down His life for us." Jesus's willingness to take on the hardship of the cross reveals the depth of His love for us. Sacrifice reveals love, and Jesus's sacrifice on the cross is the greatest display of love we could ever receive. If we ever doubt God's love for us, we only need to look at the cross.

Jesus's time in the garden also teaches us endurance and obedience in our own sufferings. We will experience suffering as believers, but we can endure suffering with the help of the Lord. Our faith can be strengthened during trials as we trust God and move forward in obedience to the Lord. As we press on in this life, we model the words of our Savior by surrendering ourselves to God with open hands saying, "Not what I will, but what You will."

If we ever doubt God's love for us, we only need to look at the cross.

What does it say about God's character that He would be willing to suffer and die for you? Meditate on John 3:16 and Galatians 2:20.

Why is prayer important in the face of trials and sufferings?
How does Jesus model the importance of prayer in this passage?

How do Jesus's obedience and endurance encourage you in your current trials and sufferings?

Jesus's kingdom, the kingdom of God, is not about power, position, or pride— it is about humility, service, and love.

The betrayal and arrest of Jesus is finally here. We can only imagine how tense this situation must be. A mob with swords and clubs suddenly surrounds Jesus. One of Jesus's disciples steps forward and kisses Jesus's cheek, designating himself as the one who has betrayed Jesus and signaling to those around him to arrest the man before him. Will Jesus resist His arrest? Will Jesus respond in retaliation?

The people around Jesus have come prepared to fight, but not Jesus. One of Jesus's own disciples even responds with force (Mark 14:47), but not Jesus. Instead, Jesus says, "the Scriptures must be fulfilled" (Mark 14:49). Jesus knows the Father's plan. He knows that the prophets have proclaimed how the Messiah would be taken by force and killed. The time has come, and Jesus accepts His arrest, fulfilling the Scriptures spoken years ago.

But how do the disciples react to Jesus's arrest? Mark tells us that they all desert Jesus and run away. Jesus's sad prediction to His disciples has come true. One of the disciples, presumably Mark himself, tries to follow Jesus. But when the mob tries to grab him, he flees while naked. The disciples' reaction reveals their fear of man. They are afraid of being arrested, accused, and possibly even killed. Yet Jesus remains firm in the face of impending death.

Jesus is first taken to the high priest in the gathering of the Sanhedrin. Mark records how the chief priests and the Sanhedrin attempt to bring testimony against Jesus, but none of them could come up with a cohesive argument. When the high priest asks why Jesus does not have an answer to these testimonies, Jesus remains silent. But when the high priest asks Jesus if He is the Messiah, Jesus replies, "I am." Jesus also adds how they will see the Son of Man seated at the right hand of God and coming on the clouds of heaven.

With this statement, Jesus combines the words of Psalm 110 and Daniel 7, two chapters of Scripture that speak to a Divine King who is equal with God and will come to judge the earth. Jesus designates Himself as this Divine King—the Messiah and the Son of Man—who is both man and divine. Jesus's bold statement of identity causes the high priest to tear his robes and declare blasphemy. It is one thing for Jesus to say that He is the Messiah, but it is another for Jesus to say that He is equal with God. Because of this supposed blasphemy, the Sanhedrin condemns Him and declares that He deserves death.

However, the Sanhedrin did not have the legal power to declare a legitimate sentence of death, so Jesus must be brought to the Roman governor, Pilate. Before Jesus is taken, the narrative shifts into the courtyard where Peter is sitting with some servants. Three times, the people around Peter accuse Peter of being Jesus's disciple, and Peter denies every claim. The sound of the rooster crowing alerts Peter to the fact that Jesus's prediction of Peter's denial has come true.

In the morning, Jesus appears before Pilate. Pilate asks Jesus, "Are you the king of the Jews?" (Mark 15:2). This question by Pilate is a question of political charge. In essence, Pilate is asking Jesus: *Are you leading the Jews in political revolt?* Jesus neither confirms nor denies Pilate's question. He only says, "You say so" (Mark 15:2). Jesus's response, as well as His constant silence to the accusations against Him, reveal to Pilate that Jesus is innocent (Mark 15:14). However, Pilate allows the crowd to decide Jesus's fate. It was customary at the time of the Passover festival for one prisoner to be released. Will Jesus be released? Or will they release the murderer Barabbas? The chief priests convince the crowd to release Barabbas. The same people who called out for Jesus to save them a few chapters earlier (Mark 11:1–11) now call out for Jesus to be killed. Barabbas is released, and Jesus is sentenced to be crucified.

We can think about the questions posed earlier. Did Jesus resist His arrest or respond with retaliation? No. Jesus prayed in the previous passage for God's will to be done, and both this arrest and crucifixion are part of God's will. Jesus does not respond with physical resistance or violence, nor does He verbally try to defend Himself against His allegations. Instead, Jesus goes willingly and remains silent, only opening His mouth with words confirming His identity. The actions of Jesus fulfill the Scriptures, specifically Isaiah 53:7, which says, "He was oppressed and afflicted, yet he did not open his mouth. Like a lamb led to the slaughter and like a sheep silent before her shearers, he did not open his mouth."

Jesus's response in His arrest and sentence reveals how Jesus is a different kind of king. He has not come to lead a revolt against the Roman government, nor does He encourage violence. Jesus has come not to enact violence but to receive violence on our behalf. Jesus's kingdom is not of this world. His actions display what Jesus has taught throughout His ministry. Jesus's kingdom, the kingdom of God, is not about power, position, or pride — it is about humility, service, and love.

Jesus's actions cause us to consider which kingdom we are embracing. Are we like the Sanhedrin, Pilate, and even Jesus's disciples, who were consumed with the kingdom of this world? Or are we like Jesus, who was dedicated to the kingdom of God, who valued God's will and ways over human agenda and affirmation? Jesus died so that we could be freed from the kingdom of this world and belong to the kingdom of God — a kingdom that is eternal rather than temporal. How we live and where we place our identity reveal which kingdom we are embracing. Which will you choose?

Jesus died so that we could be freed from the kingdom of this world and belong to the kingdom of God.

How are humility, service, and love more powerful than status or violent opposition?

Read 1 Peter 2:21—23. What does it look like to follow Jesus's example according to this passage? What does this look like practically for your everyday life?

How do you see people today living for the kingdom of this world? In what ways do you see yourself living for the kingdom of this world?

The King of kings humbles Himself by
following through with the Father's will,
even though it will cost Him His life.

Jesus's fate has been decided. He will be crucified. Though Jesus has done nothing wrong, He will face one of the most horrific forms of punishment meant for the most heinous criminals. Yet this way of death demonstrates His great humility. Jesus takes on the punishment of the lowest of the low on the cross. The King of kings humbles Himself by following through with the Father's will, even though it will cost Him His life. What dedication. What humility. What love.

The military soldiers lead Jesus to be crucified and decide to make a mockery of Jesus. They dress Him in purple robes and place a crown of thorns upon His head. They sarcastically salute Jesus and say, "Hail, king of the Jews!" and bow before Him in derision (verses 18–19). Yet the sarcasm of their homage is displayed as they beat and spit on Jesus. The military fails to honor Jesus as King. However, the irony of the military's mockery is that their words and actions confirm Jesus's identity. Jesus is the King, and although these men fail to see Jesus for who He really is, Jesus's identity remains. He is not just the King of the Jews but the King of all creation.

Jesus is then taken to the location of His crucifixion called Golgotha, which means "Place of the Skull." Jesus is stripped of His clothes, which the soldiers cast lots to claim. He is placed between two criminals on either side of Him, with a sign above His head that reads, "The King of the Jews." Those who pass by Jesus on the cross, the chief priests, and the scribes mock Jesus. They even demand Jesus to come down from the cross to prove His identity as the Son of God. While Jesus had the power to come down from the cross, He chose not to. It was the Father's will for Jesus to be crucified. By not saving Himself, Jesus would save all those who trust and believe in Him.

As time progresses, darkness begins to come over the land. Mark notes that it was noon, so this darkness was not associated with the time of day. This darkness was a strange occurrence, but it was no coincidence. Throughout Scripture, darkness represents God's judgment (Exodus 10:21). The darkness that lay over the land represents the judgment we all deserve because of our sin. This judgment involves an eternity of darkness and separation from God. However, Jesus took our judgment upon Himself on the cross. Because sin separates us from God, our sin that Jesus took on Himself causes separation between Him and God. Jesus experiences God forsaking Him, so we never will. Jesus experiences separation from God, so we can be near God.

This truth is further demonstrated as Jesus releases His last breath, and the temple curtain is torn in two. The temple curtain separated mankind from entering into the holiest area of the temple where God's presence dwelled. This supernatural happening symbolizes the access given to man by Jesus's death. Because of Jesus's sacrifice, God forgives those who trust and believe in Jesus. Our sin no longer separates us from God. We can come near our Father, and He gives us permanent access to Him—all because of Christ's sacrifice.

Mark records a significant response to Jesus's death. As a Roman centurion looks upon Jesus on the cross, he says, "Truly this man was the Son of God!" (verse 39). This Roman officer, a Gentile, is the first person to confess that Jesus is the Son of God in Mark. Many have declared that Jesus was the Messiah but not the Son of God. The centurion's reaction stands in contrast to the reactions of the other people around Jesus. While others mock Jesus as King, the centurion recognizes that Jesus is King. The other people demonstrate their unbelief by demanding that Jesus come down from the cross, but the centurion demonstrates his belief with his comment as he gazes upon Jesus on the cross.

We all have a choice: to be like those who rejected Jesus or like the centurion who received Jesus. One choice leads to darkness and death; the other leads to light and life. Jesus's death on the cross is our means for rescue. Without Jesus, we are all in the darkness of sin. The spiritual darkness symbolized by the physical darkness is what Jesus sets us free from through His death. First Peter 2:9 tells us how Jesus calls us out of darkness into His marvelous light. Rejecting Jesus keeps us in the dark, but receiving Jesus rescues us from the dark. Jesus rescues us from the darkness of our sin and brings us into the light of His mercy and grace.

Jesus not only rescues us from darkness but releases darkness's hold on us. Because of Jesus, we are free. However, we can forget this truth in our day-to-day lives. We may have been brought from death to life but forget that we daily walk in the light of Christ. When we struggle with sin or feel the weight of the sinful world, we can feel hopeless. But as believers, darkness is behind us, and light is forever before us. Even if we struggle with sin, the good news of the gospel declares that we are fully forgiven and fully free. We walk in the light of Christ now, and we will live in the light of Christ for all of eternity.

The good news of the gospel declares that we are fully forgiven and fully free.

Why is it significant that the first person to receive Christ after His death was a Gentile? Consider the temple curtain and your reflections from Week 5 Day 1 on page 117.

How does Jesus's suffering on the cross impact your own moments of suffering?

How should you respond to Jesus's death on the cross?

Only God can bring life from death.

The King of the Jews is dead. Jesus's followers likely felt hope within them die as Jesus took His last breath. But Jesus's death was not the end but the beginning. Death was only a temporary reality for Jesus. The darkness of death would soon be pierced by the light of life. Three days later, the disciples would receive the best news they could ever receive—Jesus is alive.

Three days after Jesus's death, Mary Magdalene, Mary, and Salome, who was the wife of Zebedee, journey in the early morning to Jesus's tomb. These women are expecting Jesus to be dead, and they bring with them spices to anoint Jesus's body. However, upon arriving at the tomb, they notice that the large stone covering the entrance of the tomb has been rolled away. The women see an angel inside the tomb who proclaims that Jesus is not here. Jesus is risen!

The angel tells the women to share with the disciples the news of Jesus's resurrection and how Jesus is going ahead of them to Galilee, just as He had told them (Mark 16:7). The angel's words fulfill Jesus's promise from Mark 14:28. Although the disciples have scattered and abandoned Jesus, Jesus has gone ahead of them to Galilee, where He would gather the disciples together again. The fulfillment of this promise speaks volumes of Christ's grace. The disciples have failed Jesus, but Jesus has not failed them. He would forgive the disciples' failure of faith, Peter included, and would bring them together as a testimony of His love and mercy. Jesus's grace toward them teaches us how there is no person too far gone to receive Christ's forgiveness. No matter how we have failed in our faith or obedience to God, the forgiveness of Christ, made possible through Jesus's death and resurrection, covers us.

We would imagine that the news of Christ's resurrection would bring excitement and hope for these women, but the opposite occurs. Instead of sharing with the disciples the news of Jesus's resurrection, the women flee in fear and remain silent. The women's response reflects the response of the disciples that we have seen throughout the Gospel of Mark. The fear of the disciples often hindered their faith. Even with the display of glory in front of them, they did not believe.

Throughout Mark's Gospel, Mark has consistently presented his readers with a choice. Will we be people of humility or people of pride? Will we be like the fearful disciples or the faithful centurion? Mark 16:8 also leaves us with a choice: will Christ's resurrection fill us with fear and doubt, or will Christ's resurrection fill us with joy and belief?

Unlike the women, our joy and belief can be fueled as we remember the validity of the resurrection. We may not have witnessed Christ's resurrection with our eyes, but we can know Christ's resurrection to be true in our hearts because of God's Word. Mark's Gospel has consistently pointed us to the identity and authority of Jesus as God, and the resurrection is the culmination of Mark's teaching. Only God can bring life from death. Therefore, Jesus is without a doubt the Son of God.

The power of God to bring life from death affirms that whoever repents and trusts in Jesus is also brought from death to life. The resurrection seals the salvation Jesus made possible through His death on the cross. First Corinthians 15:17 says that if Christ has not been raised, we are still in our sins. But Scripture tells us that Jesus has been raised, which gives those who believe and trust in Him the assurance that they have been rescued from the punishment of their sins. All those who believe in Jesus are brought from death to life by the forgiveness of Christ.

What does the resurrection mean for us today? Along with salvation in Christ, the resurrection proclaims that our King is alive. Right here and now, our King is ruling and reigning. For those of us in Christ, we belong to a God who is very much alive, who is with us, and who is coming back for us. The resurrection also gives us hope for the future. Because of Christ, we have the assurance that this life is not all there is. Although we live in a world marred by sin and brokenness, one day Christ will return to set all things right. We will experience the fullness of resurrection life as we will receive glorified bodies that will never be broken again.

The hope of this future resurrection fuels our joy and perseverance in the present. Death does not have a final say in our lives. The physical resurrection to come reminds us how we do not need to be afraid of death. We can experience life in the present without fear, knowing that even if we experience death — death is an entrance to life. Therefore, we can rejoice and persevere, even in moments of suffering, knowing that our eternity with Christ awaits.

The hope of the resurrection breaks through our fear and doubt. Our faith is fueled as we remember and rejoice over the truth that our God is alive. And because our God is alive, we get to experience what it means to be truly alive. As followers of Jesus, we live in light of the resurrection. We live each day with lasting joy, peace, security, and hope as we fix our hearts on this treasured truth — Jesus is alive!

We can rejoice and persevere, even in moments of suffering, knowing that our eternity with Christ awaits.

Read 1 Corinthians 15:50—58. How does Christ's resurrection give us victory?

What does it look like for you to daily live in light of the resurrection?

How can you use God's Word to help someone who does not believe in Christ's resurrection?

Even though Jesus is on the throne, we have the promise of His presence with us.

Most Bibles include a note mentioning some of the earliest manuscripts of Mark conclude with 16:8. Church tradition agrees that verses 9–20 were likely not Mark's original ending but, rather, added sometime in the second century. While these verses are likely not Mark's original ending, we can glean much from them as we finish our study of Mark.

Our study yesterday concluded with the fear and unbelief of the women at the empty tomb. Sadly, unbelief is present in today's reading as well. Verses 9–13 tell us how Jesus appeared first to Mary Magdalene. The unbelief she previously experienced at the empty tomb is now washed away as she beholds the risen Lord. However, when she reports how she had seen Jesus to the disciples, they do not believe her. When Jesus appears to two people walking on the road, the disciples do not believe their report, either.

It is not until Jesus appears to all of the remaining disciples that they finally believe. Mark tells us how Jesus rebukes the disciples for their unbelief and hardness of heart (Mark 16:14). Jesus told His disciples several times how He would rise from the dead, but they still did not believe His words nor the testimony of others. However, even with the disciples' unbelief, Jesus commissions His disciples to spread the gospel.

The decision of Jesus to still entrust His disciples with the gospel message speaks to His boundless grace. God uses His people, imperfect as they may be, to share the good news of salvation and bring the gospel to the nations. In the moments when we feel as if our sins and failures disqualify us to be used by God, we can remember it is our position with Christ that qualifies us. By Christ's grace, we belong to His kingdom, and our status in the kingdom of God assures us that no matter our sins and failures, God will still use us to accomplish His kingdom purposes.

In verses 16–18, Jesus gives His disciples two promises. First, Jesus promises that those who believe the message of the gospel will be saved, but those who do not believe will be condemned. May this be a sobering reminder to us to make evangelism a priority in our lives. The eternal destination of those around us is determined by their belief or unbelief in the gospel. We have a vital task to spread the news of the gospel in hopes that those who do not know Jesus will be saved.

Second, Jesus promises that the disciples will be given miraculous signs that point others to the power of God. With the exception of poison, all of these signs Jesus speaks of can be found in the book of Acts, which describes the spread of Christianity after Jesus's return to heaven. God used these signs in mighty ways in the early church to confirm the testimony of the apostles and to show others the power of God, just like Jesus did when He was on earth.

After these words, Jesus ascends back into heaven and sits down at the right hand of God. The King is back on His glorious throne. But even though Jesus is on the throne, we have the promise of His presence with us. Verse 20 tells us as the disciples went out and preached the gospel, the Lord worked with them. The book of Acts reveals to us how the Holy Spirit was sent to indwell believers. Each one of us who are believers in Christ has the presence of God inside of us because of the Holy Spirit. With the presence of God with us, we are fully empowered to share the good news of the gospel.

This means that in the moments we feel afraid or unequipped to share the gospel, we can remember that we have the mighty presence of God with us. God's power works within us to open blind eyes and deaf ears to the message of the gospel.

Moments in which we feel weak and unequipped to share the gospel are moments to rest in the power of God within us. Our God is with us and goes before us.

Jesus began His relationship with His disciples by beckoning them to come and follow Him. He has given them His grace for their failures and lack of faith. He has remained faithful to them even though they failed to be faithful to Him. Now, He empowers and gives His disciples the authority to beckon others to come and follow Him. This is our task as well.

For those of us in Christ, we have accepted His call to follow Him. Every day, we continue to be obedient to this call as we step forward in faith. We can move forward confidently as we remember that each step forward is one step closer to our eternal home. Though trials and troubles will come, we can remain firm in our footing as we listen to the beckoning voice of our Savior. For one day, the path we have taken to follow Jesus will finish at the gates of eternity, where we will take the hand of the One who has guided us all along.

Our God is with us and goes before us.

Why do you think the disciples did not believe the testimony of Christ's resurrection?

Why is it important to share the message of the gospel?

How does the truth that God empowers believers for evangelism encourage you in your own evangelism?

"Go into all the world and preach
the gospel to all creation."

MARK 16:15

Summarize the main points from this week's Scripture readings.

What did you observe from this week's passages about God and His character?

What do this week's passages reveal about the condition of mankind and yourself?

How do these passages point to the gospel?

How should you respond to these passages? What specific action steps can you take this week to apply them in your life?

Write a prayer in response to your study of God's Word. Adore God for who He is, confess sins He revealed in your own life, ask Him to empower you to walk in obedience, and pray for anyone who comes to mind as you study.

Jesus's Authority & Power

Throughout the Gospel of Mark, we see multiple examples of Jesus's power and authority over creation, evil and darkness, death, and disease and disorder. Here are some passages that display Jesus's power and authority over each of these things.

CREATION

The Wind and Waves Obey Jesus — Mark 4:35–41
Jesus Walks on the Water — Mark 6:45–52

EVIL & DARKNESS

Jesus Casts a Demon out of a Man — Mark 1:21–28
Jesus Casts Demons into a Herd of Pigs — Mark 5:1–13
Jesus Casts a Demon out of a Gentile Girl — Mark 7:25–30
Jesus Casts a Demon out of a Boy — Mark 9:17–27

DEATH

Jesus Raises Jairus's Daughter from the Dead — Mark 5:35–42
Jesus Resurrects Himself from the Dead — Mark 16:5–6

DISEASE & DISORDER

Jesus Heals a Leper in Galilee — Mark 1:40–44
Jesus Heals a Paralytic — Mark 2:1–12
Jesus Heals a Shriveled Hand on the Sabbath — Mark 3:1–5
Jesus Stops a Woman's Bleeding — Mark 5:25–34
Jesus Restores Hearing to a Deaf Man — Mark 7:31–37
Jesus Restores Sight to a Blind Man — Mark 8:22–26
Jesus Heals a Blind Beggar — Mark 10:46–52

"

*If anyone wants
to follow after me,
let him deny himself,
take up his cross,
and follow me.*

— MARK 8:34B —

God's power works within us to
open blind eyes and deaf ears
to the message of the gospel.

What is the Gospel?

THANK YOU FOR READING AND ENJOYING THIS STUDY WITH US! WE ARE ABUNDANTLY GRATEFUL FOR THE WORD OF GOD, THE INSTRUCTION WE GLEAN FROM IT, AND THE EVER-GROWING UNDERSTANDING IT PROVIDES FOR US OF GOD'S CHARACTER. WE ARE ALSO THANKFUL THAT SCRIPTURE CONTINUALLY POINTS TO ONE THING IN INNUMERABLE WAYS: THE GOSPEL.

We remember our brokenness when we read about the fall of Adam and Eve in the garden of Eden (Genesis 3), where sin entered into a perfect world and maimed it. We remember the necessity that something innocent must die to pay for our sin when we read about the atoning sacrifices in the Old Testament. We read that we have all sinned and fallen short of the glory of God (Romans 3:23) and that the penalty for our brokenness, the wages of our sin, is death (Romans 6:23). We all need grace and mercy, but most importantly, we all need a Savior.

We consider the goodness of God when we realize that He did not plan to leave us in this dire state. We see His promise to buy us back from the clutches of sin and death in Genesis 3:15. And we see that promise accomplished with Jesus Christ on the cross. Jesus Christ knew no sin yet became sin so that we might become righteous through His sacrifice (2 Corinthians 5:21). Jesus was tempted in every way that we are and lived sinlessly. He was reviled yet still yielded Himself for our sake, that we may have life abundant in Him. Jesus lived the perfect life that we could not live and died the death that we deserved.

The gospel is profound yet simple. There are many mysteries in it that we will never understand this side of heaven, but there is still overwhelming weight to its implications in this life. The gospel tells of our sinfulness and God's goodness and a gracious gift that compels a response. We are saved by grace through faith, which means that we rest with faith in the grace that Jesus Christ displayed on the cross (Ephesians 2:8-9). We cannot save ourselves from our brokenness or do any amount of good works to merit God's favor. Still, we can have faith that what Jesus accomplished in His death, burial, and resurrection was more than enough for our salvation and our eternal delight. When we accept God, we are commanded to die to ourselves and our sinful desires and live a life worthy of the calling we have received (Ephesians 4:1). The gospel compels us to be sanctified, and in so doing, we are conformed to the likeness of Christ Himself. This is hope. This is redemption. This is the gospel.

SCRIPTURES TO REFERENCE:

GENESIS 3:15 — *I will put hostility between you and the woman, and between your offspring and her offspring. He will strike your head, and you will strike his heel.*

ROMANS 3:23 — *For all have sinned and fall short of the glory of God.*

ROMANS 6:23 — *For the wages of sin is death, but the gift of God is eternal life in Christ Jesus our Lord.*

2 CORINTHIANS 5:21 — *He made the one who did not know sin to be sin for us, so that in him we might become the righteousness of God.*

EPHESIANS 2:8-9 — *For you are saved by grace through faith, and this is not from yourselves; it is God's gift — not from works, so that no one can boast.*

EPHESIANS 4:1-3 — *Therefore I, the prisoner in the Lord, urge you to walk worthy of the calling you have received, with all humility and gentleness, with patience, bearing with one another in love, making every effort to keep the unity of the Spirit through the bond of peace.*

Thank you for studying
God's Word with us!

CONNECT WITH US

@thedailygraceco
@dailygracepodcast

CONTACT US

info@thedailygraceco.com

SHARE

#thedailygraceco

VISIT US ONLINE

www.thedailygraceco.com

MORE DAILY GRACE

The Daily Grace App
Daily Grace Podcast